"I love the Anglo-American tales; the[y] experience of being in the US, for it t[...] We can communicate but we are so [...] these poems. A chance to travel witho[ut ...ming the environment:] .
**Ros Fry**
West Mead Creative, Founder: Dorset Literature Live

"Sumptuous stuff – evocative, provocative and insightful."
**Subathra Subramaniam**
Artistic Director: Sadhana, Co-Director of Education: Cape Farewell

"What unifies the varied content of these poems and prose pieces is the intelligence, the eye for telling detail and compassion of the writer. Chris Fogg takes us on a magical, whirlwind tale of his world – which means the world as a whole, through time and space. We are in Mali, in India, on the streets of New York City – on foot or roller-blade, plane, train or boat – and always with eyes and ears open and heart at full throttle. Although there is much to admire here, I can't help having a special fondness for his Anglo-American tales: "The Skater from New England", "The Waitress from Mass MoCA", "The Day The Earth Stood Still" and others, which reflect his life-long romance with the USA. He loves us, and we can't help loving back, even if we're not quite sure we deserve it. His very best, lyrical passion, however, is in some of the quieter, more personal work: the horse with its chestnut mane prefiguring the long red hair of his beloved wife, Amanda, whom we later see in a moment of utter felicity, kneeling in her garden and looking up, radiant. Here is a collection to be read, if you can, at a breathless sitting, and savoured."
**Irene Willis**
Pushcart Poetry Prize nominee and Winner of the Violet Reed Haas Award

'So I swallowed my swozzle and sought my own voice...'
(No More Heroes)
"This collection is rich with that found voice. Whether re-tracing family memory, or travelling through other cultures and encountering other lives, that voice is consistently observant, empathetic, celebratory, elegaic – and challenging. These poems are freewheeling but crafted despatches from a lived life, taking the pulse of how-it-is, and joyfully engaging with their cultural contexts. They cut an arc across our times – they are travels of the heart, and invite us to travel with them."
**Chris Waters**
Winner of Bridport and Plough Poetry Prizes, author of Arisaig

## Plays by Chris Fogg

The Tall Tree*
To See The Six Points*
[* *with music by Chris Dumigan*]
The Silent Princess
Changeling
Flotsam & Jetsam
Peterloo: The Greatest Show On Earth
Snapshot  [*co-written with Andrew Pastor & Chris Phillips*]
Safe Haven
Firestarter
Trying To Get Back Home
Heroes
Bogus
It's Not Just The Jewels…
You Are Harry Kipper & I Claim My Five Pounds!
One of Us**
How To Build A Rocket**
[** *co-written with Gavin Stride*]

For young people and community companies:
The Ballad of Billy The Kid
Small Blue Thing
Market Forces
Inside
The Sleeping Clock
Titanic
The Posy Tree
Scheherezade
Persons Reported

Adaptations:
1984
(In The Land Of) Zorn
Return of the Native
The Stone Book Quartet
The Birdman

Musical Theatre:
Stag***
Marilyn***
[*** *co-written with Chris Dumigan*]

Chris Fogg is a creative producer who has written and directed for the theatre for many years, as well as more recently offering dramaturgical advice and support for choreographers and dance companies.

**Special Relationships**
is his first collection of poems.

# Special Relationships

## poems and stories by Chris Fogg

mudlark

First published by Mudlark Press 2011
in a limited edition of 500
© Chris Fogg 2010

ISBN 978-0-9565162-3-7

Printed in Exeter by Short Run Press Ltd
Cover and design by
Sally Chapman-Walker

Published and distributed by
Mudlark Press, Littlehempston, Devon
www.mudlarkpress.co.uk

Front cover image:
© 2011 Classic Media, LLC.
THE LONE RANGER and associated
character names, images and other
indicia are trademarks of and copyrighted
by Classic Media, LLC.
All rights reserved.

The extract from the song
*Looking For A New England* in
*The Skater From New England*
is reproduced by kind permission of
Billy Bragg.

The reference to a "dance at a slight
angle to the universe" in Section 9 of
*The Day The Earth Stood Still* appears by
kind courtesy of Ben Wright, Artistic
Director of the dance company *bgroup*,
in whose recent production *About Around*
this dance was performed.
www.bgroup.org.uk

for Amanda & Tim

# Special Relationships
## Contents

### Ripping Up The Past 1 — 1
| | |
|---|---|
| Alison Smiling | 2 |
| Ripping Up The Past | 3 |
| Kidsongs | 6 |
| Rites of Passage | 10 |
| The Boy in the Wardrobe | 12 |
| Cricket Bats | 26 |

### Lost Empires
#### 1. India — 31
| | |
|---|---|
| Hero Cyclist | 32 |
| Bombay Film Poster | 34 |
| A Chance Encounter | 35 |
| Vinoba and the Three Brothers | 37 |
| Bharat Mata | 39 |
| Sophie & Gita | 43 |

### Lost Empires
#### 2. Mali — 47
| | |
|---|---|
| Land Cruisers | 48 |
| Fly Blown In Douantzé | 52 |
| Statistics (Lies, Damned Lies and…) | |
| The Top Ten Countdown | 54 |
| Poi | 60 |
| Crossing the Niger | 61 |
| One For The Wallet | 64 |
| Patric Takes A Photograph | 66 |
| Dogon Country | 68 |
| Le Bel Oiseau Bleu | 82 |

## The Special Relationship
**Three Anglo-American Tales**    83
The Waitress From Mass. MoCA    84
The Businessman From Buffalo    89
The Skater From New England    99

## Ripping Up The Past 2    119
The Unconsidered Things    120
A Folk Play    121
Coming of Age    125
Horse in the Yard    127
First Night Nerves    128
Acting Class    129
When Dad First Died    132
Getting the Knack    133

## The Day The Earth Stood Still    135
1 - 10    136

## Ripping Up The Past 3    173
No More Heroes    174
Family Trees    176
Google Earth    179
Moon Magic    181
Potting On    183

*And out of his grave grew a red, red rose,*
*And out of hers, a briar.*

*They grew and grew in the old churchyard,*
*Till they couldn't grow no higher,*
*They lapped and tied in a true love's knot.*
*The rose ran around the briar.*

         *Barbara Allen Traditional*

*

*This means a special relationship between the British Commonwealth and Empire and the United States*
         Winston Churchill

*All that remains of the 'special relationship' is really a ball and chain limiting our capacity to play a more positive role in the world.*
         Tony Benn

*It's not just a backward-looking or nostalgic relationship*
         William Hague (to Hillary Clinton)

*We celebrate a common heritage. We cherish common values.*
         Barack Obama

*

*(It's) only a northern song…*
         George Harrison

# Ripping Up the Past

**1**

## Alison Smiling

"You're just an old hippy at heart,"
she said, a twinkle in her eye,
"a romantic, nostalgic, boring old fart –
the present is passing you by.
It's the new millennium, didn't you know?
Not 1968..."
She picked up her books and turned to go,
knowing I'd rise to the bait.

"All I meant was: do what Brecht did –
plunder the past, and then reject it."
She looked me straight in the eye:
"If you really believe that's why you teach,
why don't you practise what you preach?"
I couldn't answer her why.

\*

Later I thought, it's true what she said
(while sorting through tired old lesson notes):
if I want to proclaim that the past is dead,
why do I teach in anecdotes?
Why do I cling like a drowning man
to the past like wreckage that bobs and floats
tossing me, washing me up where I ran
from – a wound that will not be bled?

Time, like a boomerang, has the knack
of suddenly, painfully, hurtling back –
a kestrel above a motorway
hovering relentlessly seeking its prey,
a lazy, seductive glide, then a pounce,
like Alison smiling with exit-line flounce.

## Ripping Up the Past

I found my gran in gleeful mood
in the gleaming, steaming kitchen; the smell
of beetroots on the boil; home-preserved food
in sealed jars crammed shelves on every wall,
and there, in the centre of it all,
singing while the rhubarb stewed,
my gran was ripping photographs.
                                          A bagful
lay on the floor already. "Would
you watch," she asked, in mid-atonic phrase,
"where you put your feet? I'm sorting…"
Then over to the oven to pull out trays
of scones: "For tea," she warned then, noting
my expression, scraped together broken
crumbs to stuff my fists. "These
can go an' all," she said, "courting
snaps of me and Hubert, days
long gone…" Weddings, Whit-Walks,
cousins' christenings: wide-eyed,
appalled, I watched her toss Works'
Outings, Cricket Teas, Church Fêtes I'd
heard so much about… *Abide
With Me* welled up while cakes
were brushed and nutmeg coated
on to warm egg custards. Flakes
of pastry fell like snow and
settled on the fading sepia,
a film on film, like a gloved hand
across the eye.

                         That noise of paper
tearing cut the kitchen, drowned
the other normal daily sounds
of song and simmering. A shower
of memories like peelings piled beside her.

"Why?" I wailed. The singing stopped,
she gripped my shoulder hard. "I've
done with 'em," she said, then tapped

her temple. "All in here." She gave
me her old-fashioned stare. "Have
you learned nowt at school?" A blackbird hopped
up on the window-sill, a look of
cold compliance in its eyes. From gran's cupped
palm it pecked some seeds. "Is it tame?"
I whispered. "Don't be daft – why should it
be?" The window clouded up with steam,
her fingers fountained, the bird twisted
in reluctant flight, shook its ragged frame
and, like me, was gone, as if it never came.
Would it return tomorrow? Ever? Would it?

I held that moment then; I had it,
I thought, frozen, trapped, unchanging;
but the years trick me – did it happen,
or did I just imagine
it, filling in details to force open
a long-closed door? Do snapshots cage in
memory or unlock it?
       Occasion-
-ally my gran's would falter, hearken
back to reminiscences, uncertain
of a fact or two. "When I was a girl,"
she'd say, "I sang a lot. I had boys
eating from my hand. They all
thought I had the loveliest voice.
At parties – such excitement, such noise –
I checked my music, made my choice…
Most of them are dead now, a whole
generation gone – Tommy, Jim,
so many… What use are these?"
She tossed another bundle in the bin,
her fingers lightly trembling on her thighs
the rhythm of a favourite chapel hymn,
she sang, her voice now quavery and thin…

Outside the door another blackbird flies,
alights as I remember, and takes wing.

"Out with the old, a new broom..."
She burned a thousand photographs that day
and still I wonder why I feel the loss
so keenly. Is it the act, or the sure way
she threw each memory so casually away
that makes me down the years still cross?
"Photographs are lies," she said. "They
freeze time when I'd rather let it pass...
and besides, they take up too much room."

## Kidsongs

> *intery mintery cutery corn*
> *apple seed and apple thorn*
> *wire briar limber lock*
> *three fat geese in a flock*
> *one flew east and one flew west*
> *and one flew over the cuckoo's nest*

This is the story about the Picks
Mum and Dad and seven kids
Billy and Sheila, John and Doreen
David and Brian (the twins) and Kathleen
Mum was enormous with nicotined grin
Dad was dapper, downtrodden and thin
He kept an allotment as tidy as a mouse
And they all lived together in a tiny terraced house

> *the big ship sails down the ally-ally-o*
> *the ally-ally-o, the ally-ally-o*
> *the big ship sails down the ally-ally-o*
> *on the last day of September*

This is the story of Doreen Pick
Who had to get married double-quick
The wedding reception was held in the chippy
But her husband-to-be proved equally nippy
He ran away, never more to be seen
Saddled Doreen with a kid at 16

> *the king of Spain's daughter*
> *said she'd marry me*
> *and all for the sake of*
> *my little nut tree*

This is the story of Big John Pick
Strong as an ox and thick as a brick
He'd play with an orange for most of each day
Till the hated Miss Brown came and snatched it away
Gloating she flung it into the stove
Triumphant she taunted him till she drove

Him so wild he plunged his arm in
Right up to the elbow and scalded the skin
Big John Pick was beside himself
He hoisted Miss Brown to the top of a shelf
A terrible silence there then ensued
Till somebody roared, then as one devilish brood
We raced to the playground a-rocking and reeling
Leaving Miss Brown a-kicking and squealing

> *bat bat come under my hat*
> *and I'll give you a slice of bacon*
> *and when I bake I'll give you some cake*
> *unless I'm much mistaken*

This is the story of Billy Pick
Who ate his own shit and was violently sick
At the age of eleven he still acted four
He liked to push plasticine through knot-holes in the floor
Poor Billy Pick never learned to talk
He spluttered and slobbered as though chewing chalk
His National Health specs were wound round with plaster
He tripped over bootlaces – a walking disaster
Always the butt of our cruellest games
We teased him, tormented him, called him rude names –
But one day Billy Pick counted to ten
We asked him to do it again and again
His face broke out in the broadest of beams
A sunflower-sandman-smiler of dreams
This broken, lolling puppet-like boy
Moon-faced, transfigured, to absolute joy
We carried him shoulder high round the school
King for a Day, the Feast of the Fool…
I'll always remember the dinner-time when
Billy Pick counted from one up to ten

> *if wishes were horses*
> *beggars would ride*
> *if turnips were watches*
> *I'd wear one by my side*

This is the story of Sheila Pick
On whom Life played the meanest trick
She was the exception that proves the rule
Clever and pretty, the family's jewel
A university place beckoned maybe
But she had to stay home and help Mum with each baby…

> *little Periwinkle*
> *with her eyes a-twinkle*
> *said – "I'm going to the ball tonight"*
> *but nobody could wake her*
> *hard as they might shake her*
> *her eyes were shut so tight*

Kathleen would never say boo to a goose
She clung to her mum and would never let loose
This is the story of young Kathleen –
Went the same way as her sister Doreen…
David and Brian (identical twins)
"They've put them both in loony bins" –
(Because they refused to co-operate)
(Because they never would separate)
"They've committed no crime except being born" –
Mrs Pick had nothing but scorn
For the social workers' authority
"All they want's to split up my family" –
But none of the kids got taken away
Just another slice of life in this kitchen-sink play
Dad kept growing his prize-winning flowers
While Mum lay awake in the early hours…

> *shoe the horse and shoe the mare*
> *don't let the little colt go bare*
> *one two three four five six seven*
> *all good children go to heaven*

\*

Inner city or stuck in the sticks
Every school's got its family of Picks

Now my son's at a small church school
With its fair share of jokers, eccentrics and fools
He comes back occasionally asking odd
Questions about the nature of God
Is God a woman? White or black?
Is God in the zip of my anorak?
At first I don't answer, then after a while
I say: if God exists anywhere it's in Billy Pick's smile

## Rites of Passage

Behind the schoolyard, between the steel works
and the embankment, lay the bomb-site:
a ruin of mattresses, heaped bricks, dumped tyres;
a tangle
of wrecked cars, bed-springs, rusty wires.
Into this jungle
we boys plunged, to smoke and write
rude words about the gaudy girls
who coiled their fingers round their curls
and taunted us with threats of sex –

blown kisses, flashed knickers – then a shriek
as they fled towards the railway track
to blow away time on dandelion clocks,
their laughter
stinging us like electric shocks.
After
these preliminaries came the ac-
-tual initiation rite
itself – a dare? a fight? –
spilling blood to join their clique.

When my turn came I had to walk across
a plank suspended over a lime pit
where rats the size of tom-cats lurked –
you scored
extra if it bounced or jerked.
My reward,
if ever I dared to do it,
was to be ceremonially led,
blindfold, towards the cycle shed
where waiting for me was Margaret Ness.

Margaret, Margaret Ness, whose dimpled cheeks, shy smile
broke a hundred hearts. My classmate George
and I fought for her through a whole playtime,
dislodging
the stacked coke-pile till she came
watching

us with a look I couldn't gauge...
Then one week after finishing school
George drowned in a crowded swimming pool –
I read it in *The Daily Mail*.

\*

The steel works shut down. There are no bomb-sites
now. The school's all boarded up. Weeds clog
the playground. I've not seen Margaret since.

Finding
years later our initials on a fence
reminded
me: the past looks different when it's dug
up. Like archaeologists we pin on names,
misinterpret the unearthed remains,
best left covered by the new estates.

## The Boy in the Wardrobe

He'd been sent to his room by his grandmother. "You've disappointed your grandfather," she'd said. "You've let him down." *He* hadn't said this, *she* had. And she was right, and the boy knew it. But he hadn't gone to his bedroom. He knew that there he would just look out of the window. Like as not the girl from across the way would be sitting on her window-sill, looking out too, when she was supposed to be doing her homework. Julie. That was her name, though he had never spoken to her, just waved. His friend Michael said he'd seen her kissing his brother Terry in the bus shelter one day after school. He didn't know what he felt about that. He'd never kissed anyone yet, except for his family, and when anyone kissed on the TV he'd turn away, embarrassed. Like his grandmother. "Stop it," she'd call out to the television, "and get on with the story." So he knew that if he looked across now and caught her eye, he'd wave, and then blush, and he would forget about disappointing his grandfather. And he didn't want to forget. He wanted to think about what he had done. And so he had crept into his grandparents' room and stolen into the wardrobe, where it was completely dark, and he could be quite alone, without any distractions. And that was where he was now, crouched in a corner, beneath the overcoats hanging above him, the smell of mothballs somehow a comfort, as his cheeks burned red and hot with shame. He had lied.

After a few minutes he heard footsteps in the hallway. He recognised them at once as his grandfather's, who had a slower tread than his grandmother, who never went anywhere without bustling. He heard him go into his bedroom and call his name. Then – "Annie…? He's not here. Where do you think he's gone? You don't think he's run off, do you?"

"Here, let me," said his grandmother, brushing past his grandfather with a flick of her tea towel. "Typical. That boy, he'll be the death of me. Don't worry, Hubert. I know exactly where he'll be." And in an instant he could hear her approaching the wardrobe. "Don't think I don't know where you are, my lad. Come out this minute." And she flung open the door. He tried to make himself as small as possible, but it was no use. His grandmother had X-ray eyes, which could pierce even her darkest fur coat, and as the light from the window edged towards him, he shot out like a greyhound from a trap and dashed back to his bedroom. "He always hides in there," she said. "He thinks I don't know."

At once he could hear his grandfather sigh. "Haven't you punished him enough, Annie? Let me have a word with him." Mercifully she told him to leave the boy be, to go into the kitchen and help her with shelling the peas. They went, and he let out a long, slow breath. Facing his grandfather would have been much worse than his grandmother's quick temper. He would have simply sat there, held his hand, and asked him what was the matter. And his heart would have burst.

After a while, his grandmother opened the bedroom door, looked down on the boy, and said, "Come on, Christopher. Your tea's ready. It's bangers and mash, with peas, your favourite." She smiled, ruffled the top of his head, then added, "We'll say no more about it," and he followed her into the kitchen, where his grandfather sat waiting. He was peeling an apple.

"Oh," said Christopher, "aren't you having any tea?"

"He's got his meeting," his grandmother replied. "I expect he'll have something when he gets back."

"We'll see," he said, still peeling the apple. "We don't want any fuss, do we? There – look." He held up the apple-peel.

"You've done it," the boy cried, "in one single go!" His eyes were full of wonder.

Granddad came towards him. "Go feed it to that blackbird you're so fond of."

"His tea'll get cold."

"After his tea then."

"If he's good."

"Oh – he'll be good," and he dropped the peeling lightly onto the top of the dresser, and winked at him. "I'll be off then, Annie. I shan't be late."

"Mind you take your scarf. You don't want that cold on your chest again." And he was gone.

The clock in the kitchen ticked in the silence between them, as his grandmother took off her pinny and sat down opposite him.

"Now then," she said, as he chased the last pea around

13

his plate, "are you going to tell me what all this has been about?"

"Sorry, Nanna," he said.

"Sorry won't fix things now, will it?"

"But I am – truly."

"I daresay. And I daresay your tummy's better too, seeing as how you've wolfed down your tea."

He looked down at his empty plate. "Yes, Nanna."

"Well don't think you're having any of that chocolate cake I baked this morning."

"No, Nanna."

The clock ticked on, while his grandmother wordlessly began to hum one of her favourite chapel hymns, her voice quavery and thin. The cat strolled into the kitchen from the garden and, instantly sizing up the situation, proceeded to wind himself around his grandmother's ankles.

"And I suppose you want feeding now too?"

The cat mewed obligingly, while his grandmother got up, put her pinny back on and fetched the tin of cat meat from the pantry shelf.

"I'll wash up then, shall I?" the boy asked.

"Don't think you can get round me that way, but all right – you can dry." And she tossed him the tea towel with the picture of the Welsh Lady on it, then carried on singing her hymn.

Afterwards, on a normal day, he would have gone out for a last game of cricket with Michael on the field. But today was not a normal day, and Michael was a part of the problem. Then he would have come in and perhaps played cards with his grandparents, or scrabble, before a mug of hot chocolate and then bed. Tonight his grandmother said, "Well, I think there's been enough excitement for one day, don't you? How about an early night?"

Christopher knew there was no arguing, and so off he went to clean his teeth and get ready for bed. A few minutes later his grandmother came into his room, drew the curtains, and looked down on him. "Say your prayers, then try to sleep, all right?"

"Yes, Nanna. I'm sorry."

"I know you are. Now think on what you've done, and

tomorrow we'll start afresh, eh? Goodnight."

She closed the door and he tried to say his prayers, but it was difficult, for he always pictured God as looking rather like his grandfather, and he knew he didn't want to look into that face and see those kind, forgiving eyes, not tonight. He turned over and began to look back at the events of the day…

\*

It had all started the night before, when he'd been round at Michael's. He and his brother Terry were telling jokes, privately to one another, and giggling. Christopher knew that the jokes would be dirty, about sex, and that he wouldn't understand them, and that that would only make the other two laugh even more. He wished Terry would go out and leave him alone with Michael. Mike was always great when it was just the two of them. They both shared the same passion for cricket and could talk about it, when they were not actually playing, agreeably for hours. But when Terry was around, Michael acted differently, tougher, meaner, like he was trying to impress. Everyone liked Terry. He was clever and funny, good at sport, polite to grown-ups, liked by girls. But he was two years older than Mike and Christopher, and next to him, he always felt a baby.

Suddenly Terry was by his side, with his head in an armlock. "When do you go back, squirt?"

"In about half an hour."

"Not tonight, squirt – back home, to your parents?"

"Oh." Christopher didn't like to think about that. He came to stay with his grandparents every school holiday. This summer he had already been here for over six weeks, and he knew that soon it would be time to go back. It was like when you turned over an hour glass. At first there was so much sand it felt like it would never run out. Then, when it neared the bottom, it all seemed to rush out at once.

Oi, squirt!" said Terry, rubbing his fist along the top of his head. "I asked you a question."

"Tuesday."

Surprisingly Terry let him go. It was as if for a brief

moment he didn't want Christopher to go either. "That's a pity. Mike'll be sorry."

Michael rolled his eyes.

"And so will I," added Terry, wrestling Christopher to the floor and pummelling him with a cushion. "Tell you what. Why don't we all go down to the beach early tomorrow morning? The tide will be out, and it should be great for a game of cricket."

Christopher looked at Terry in wonder. He had never asked him to go anywhere before, not even to tag along. "What's the matter – lost your tongue? Say yes before I change my mind."

"Yes," he gasped, and Terry let him go.

"Get lost then, and we'll see you tomorrow."

Christopher ran up the passage that linked Michael's house with his grandparents', whooping like a cowboy. When he got home, his grandmother looked up from her darning, laughing. "Well somebody's happy," she said. "Look at the state of you – shirt tucked out, hair standing on end. Whatever have you been up to?"

"Nothing much."

"How boys get into such a mess doing 'nothing much' beats me. Now – get ready for your bath, it's chapel tomorrow…"

Inwardly Christopher froze. Oh no. He'd forgotten. It was Sunday tomorrow, and Sunday meant chapel. Always. With his grandfather. Early in the morning they'd catch the bus to Colwyn Bay, to the chapel where his grandfather was a lay preacher, then they'd walk all the way back, along the promenade, arriving back in time for a Sunday lunch of roast potatoes that his grandmother would have ready for them. It was the only thing expected of him while he stayed with them. The rest of the time he was free to play all day long. But on Sundays he went to chapel.

"You've gone quiet all of a sudden," said his grandmother. "You're not sickening for something, are you?"

Maybe that was what put the idea into his head. "I don't know. My tummy hurts."

"Come to think of it, you do look a bit hot. You're not getting a temperature, I hope. Here – take a spoonful of cod liver oil and you'll be as right as rain in the morning."

He dutifully swallowed the noxious mixture, then took himself off for his bath. Once in bed he shut his eyes tight and groaned. How could he have been so stupid to forget that tomorrow was Sunday? But how could he let Mike and Terry down when he'd promised? He could already hear Terry taunting him, "Ah, does baby have to go to church with Grandpops? Ah, diddums..." How would that make him look in Michael's eyes? But how could he in all conscience not go to chapel with his grandfather?

He continued to toss and turn, unable to make up his mind. Perhaps at this rate he really would be ill tomorrow. That would get him out of chapel, but it would also prevent him from going to the beach.

Slowly sleep came, and the next thing he knew was the sound of the kettle whistling in the kitchen, and his grandmother's voice asking him if he was awake yet, and not to forget that he still hadn't brushed his shoes. "Goodness me – look at the state of your bed, it's like a jumble sale."

He dredged himself up from the pit of sleep feeling more tired and worried than when he'd gone to bed. A stone lay heavy in his stomach. He wasn't ill, he knew that, but nor was he any nearer to solving what he would do. He washed and dressed and went into the kitchen, where his grandmother had lined up his and his grandfather's Sunday shoes on a newspaper near the door. It seemed to take an age to clean them, polishing them until he could almost see his reflection in them, but at least the task had occupied his thoughts for a further fifteen minutes.

He washed his hands and sat at the table while his grandmother brought him his porridge and a boiled egg. He could see his grandfather in the hall, standing before the mirror, combing his hair with a brush in each hand. He put on his jacket, then joined the others in the kitchen, tapping the barometer in the doorway before sitting down.

"Hmm... It says it might rain. But looking at the sky we might be all right. With luck we'll be able to walk back by the sea as usual. What do you think?"

"I think you should take an umbrella," said Annie, "and then you should take the bus."

His grandfather winked towards him. "Christopher?" But he found he could say nothing.

"What's the matter with you?" asked his grandmother. "Cat got your tongue? And you haven't touched your breakfast."

"What is it, Chris? Are you not feeling yourself this morning? Come on, eat up – that'll soon put you right."

"I'm not hungry, Granddad. Honest. I can't eat it."

"You'd better eat it," said his grandmother, pushing the porridge bowl back towards him. "There'll be nothing till lunch if you don't."

"I'm sorry, Nanna. I can't."

"Can't eat was made to eat and..."

"Now then, Annie, he does look a bit peaky. Perhaps you'd better stop at home this morning, if you're coming down with something."

"And what am I supposed to do with him under my feet all day?"

"I'll tell you what, Christopher – why don't you go into my study and look at my atlases? You'd like that, wouldn't you?"

"Yes, Granddad."

"And you wouldn't get in your Nanna's way, would you?"

"No, Granddad."

"That's settled then, eh Annie?"

"You spoil him, that's what."

"Better safe than sorry. You know how cold and draughty it gets in chapel."

Christopher nodded silently, looking up at his grandmother.

"All right then. But I still want to see you eating some breakfast, understand?"

"Yes, Nanna," and he proceeded to eat his porridge obediently.

"Good lad," said his Granddad. "Right. I'd best be off." He put on his grey Abercrombie overcoat and picked up his umbrella.

"Don't forget your hat, Hubert."

"Thank you, Esther Hannah," he said, using her Sunday name. "I won't be late. No point in walking back without Christopher. I'll get the bus straight home."

Annie waved him goodbye and, as soon as he had

turned the corner, she was back in the kitchen, standing beside the boy.

"Now then, young man," she said. "What's all this about?"

He gulped. He could pull the wool over his Granddad's eyes, but never his Nanna's. Hers never missed a trick. "What do you mean?" he said.

"You know very well what I mean, Frank Fanackapan. Now get yourself off into Granddad's study and read those atlases. He'll want to know which maps you've been looking at when he gets home."

"Yes, Nanna." And off he went.

Granddad's study was his favourite room in the house. As well as the atlases, which had fascinated Christopher for as long as he could remember, it was full of all kinds of unusual and interesting things, all of which had a story. His grandfather had been a printer before he retired, and in a drawer in the bureau he kept a set of old wooden printing blocks. Christopher liked to trace the patterns of the letters carved into each block. Normally he would have loved to have been allowed to spend time in there on his own. But not this morning. His head was too full of the confused thoughts that were whizzing round his brain like racing cars on a grand prix circuit. He had managed to get out of going to chapel. His grandfather had not seemed to mind, had encouraged him in fact to rest, which made him feel worse, because, while he had not exactly told an outright lie, he'd certainly not been completely honest, had he? And what was to be gained from not going to chapel if he couldn't instead go out to the beach to play cricket with Michael and Terry? He picked up one of the printing blocks and turned it over in his fingers. It took him back to when he was much younger, before his grandfather had retired, when his grandparents lived across the road from the printing works, and how he would spend several nights a week there while his mum and dad went out dancing. He would fall asleep to the deep rumble of the giant printing machines that turned throughout the night. "Your mother used to like that sound too," his Nanna told him. "When she was a girl she'd dance to the different rhythms they'd all make. And she's not stopped dancing since." Christopher smiled. He picked up a different printing block, remembering how once he'd seen his parents dancing the jive, and the whole dance floor had cleared to watch them.

Suddenly the telephone rang, jolting him back to the present. In the study the telephone was one of those heavy, old fashioned hand-sets, all in black, while in the hall was a much more modern one – cream and slim-lined with a bleep instead of a ring. He heard his grandmother pick up that phone and then – he was never quite sure what prompted him to do this – he lifted up the old black receiver in the study and listened in.

"2587..."

"Hello, Annie. It's Florrie here. I've had a bit of an accident. I was tending to Gordon and I left the tap running in the basin upstairs and it's overflowed. It's made ever such a mess, and I could clean it up, but Gordon needs me to see to him..."

"Don't you worry yourself, love, I'll be round in a minute..."

Florrie was married to his grandfather's brother, Uncle Gordon, who was an invalid, and who you always had to be quiet around. Christopher was just replacing the receiver as his grandmother burst in.

"I've got to go to your Auntie Florrie's. I'll be about half an hour, I should think. Do you want to come with me? Or will you be all right here on your own for a bit?"

"Oh, I'll be fine here, Nanna. You go."

"Right then. Mind you don't touch anything electric."

"I won't..." And she was gone.

Not stopping to pause for breath even, Christopher watched his grandmother disappear round the corner, then dashed to the back door, where he picked up his cricket bat and, without a further thought, ran down the passage-way towards Michael and Terry's house, just as they were coming out into the road.

"We thought you weren't coming," said Michael.

"I said I would."

"Hey, squirt – what's that you've got?"

Christopher proudly held his cricket bat towards Terry.

"What on earth's that?"

"My granddad made it. It's special."

And indeed it was. They had chosen the wood carefully together, then his grandfather had fashioned the bat – blade and handle – out of the single piece. To Christopher it was wondrous, unique, special.

"Call that a cricket bat?" (Terry again). "It's just a plank of wood with a hole in the middle." He turned to Michael and clipped him across the ear. "I told you we should have brought yours – at least that looks like a cricket bat."

Michael wheeled away from the blow and hissed at Christopher, "God, you're so embarrassing."

"Oh well, we'll have to make the best of it, I suppose," said Terry, but then his attention was suddenly drawn towards two girls walking towards them along the promenade from the opposite direction. "Hello, ladies. Looks like your lucky day."

The girls giggled and tottered on towards them. "Don't fancy yours," whispered Michael to Terry.

"That's more like it, Mickey, my boy," laughed Terry. "Well girls, isn't this nice? The two of you, and the two of us. Going anywhere special?"

"Might be," said the taller of the two girls. "What's it to you?"

"Well we just happen to know somewhere very special." And in an instant the four of them coupled off, arm in arm, and began to walk away in the opposite direction from Christopher. "Oi, squirt – I don't think we'll be needing this after all," said Terry, and he tossed the bat disdainfully over his shoulder onto the rocks below them. Just then it started to rain. "Oh dear," said Terry. "Got an umbrella, girls?"

"Does it look like we have?"

"Well we know just the place, don't we, Mickey boy? There's a bus shelter just across the road. Tucked away behind the trees, it's…. what's the word, Mickey?"

"Private, Terry."

"That's it, Corporal. Private."

"Sounds nice," said the taller girl.

"Then let us escort you."

Christopher watched them walk away, then jumped down to pick up his bat. It was broken, right at the point where the handle joined the blade. He'd have to try and fix it before his grandfather saw it.

He turned towards home and wondered whether his

Nanna would be back yet from his Auntie Florrie's. With luck she'd have stayed for a cup of tea, and he would be back before she realised he'd been gone. What would he do about his wet clothes, though? For the rain was now bouncing off the road.

The answer came soon enough. Just as he turned into the road where his grandparents lived, he saw his grandmother waiting in the porch. "Where've *you* been, my lad? I've been worried sick. I came back from Florrie's and you weren't here, not even a note, you could have been kidnapped for all I knew, then you turn up looking like a drowned rat. Where've you been anyway? No, don't tell me – I can see – you've got your cricket bat with you – you've been playing with Michael, haven't you? I thought you were supposed to be poorly, eh? Too poorly for chapel, but fit enough to play cricket. Well, you ought to be ashamed of yourself. Not only have you worried me half to death, but you've lied to your Grandfather. How do you think that's going to make him feel? Honestly, Christopher, he asks nothing of you, but you know he likes you to go to chapel with him – is that too much to ask?"

"No, Nanna. I'm sorry."

"Oh, it's easy to say you're sorry now, isn't it, but the damage is done. And you can stop your crying right now. Crying's not going to do you any good. I'll give you something to really cry about in a minute. Now get to your room, change out of those wet things, and think about what you've done."

\*

The next morning the rain had stopped. The sun streamed through the curtains, waking Christopher from an empty, dreamless sleep. He got up and looked out of the window. As usual, the blackbird was sitting on the window-sill, almost as if he had been waiting.

"I shan't see you after tomorrow. Back to home and back to school."

He yawned and stretched. He felt all right, surprisingly, as though the emotions of yesterday had left him completely drained. He went into the kitchen where his grandmother was frying bacon. He knew that no more would be said about it.

"Sleep well?"

"Yes, thanks."

"Good lad. Here," she added, putting a plate of bacon sandwiches in front of him, "this'll put hairs on your chest."

After a while, his grandfather came in from the allotment at the back of his garden. "Nice morning, Christopher. What are your plans?"

"I don't have any."

"What? No plans on your last full day here?"

"Well – I thought I'd wait to see what you two were doing."

Hubert looked at Annie, who smiled and then turned away back to the sink. "Are you not playing cricket? It's a fine day for it."

"But what about you? Don't you have to go into Llandudno this morning? Maybe I could go with you?"

"Oh, I'm only going to the bank. That's not much fun for you, is it? No – you go and see if Michael's about. I expect he'll be waiting for you."

"Are you sure?"

"Well," said his grandmother, "if you'd rather stay here with me, I'm sure I could find some chores for you…"

"No thanks." Laughing, Christopher ducked under her outstretched, soapy arms and headed for the porch, where he saw his cricket bat – the special one his Granddad had made for him – lying against the door, and he stopped. "Granddad, have you got any string?"

"I expect so. Now what would you want that for?"

"Oh – I thought… I thought I'd bind it round the handle – like Gary Sobers does."

"Well if that's how Gary Sobers has it," said Granddad, smiling, "you'd best do the same. Follow me. There'll be some string in the shed, I shouldn't wonder."

Five minutes later Christopher was walking down the drive, opening the gate, then heading towards the passageway that led up to Michael's house. Just before he reached it, however, he stopped and sat on the wall. What if Michael doesn't want to see him, he thought? What if Terry's hanging around? What if they start teasing him again?

"Penny for them?"

"What?"

"Your thoughts." It was Julie. The girl from across the way. "You looked miles away."

"I will be soon. I'm going back tomorrow."

"That's a shame. But you'll be back at half term, won't you? That's not long, is it? Six weeks? My mum says I can have a Halloween party. Would you like to come?"

Christopher shrugged. "Maybe."

"You're funny." Then she smiled at him sideways and pecked him on the cheek.

Christopher's jaw practically hit the floor.

"What's up? Never been kissed before? How about a proper one?"

Christopher's face went the colour of beetroot.

"I'm not going to ask you twice!"

"No thank you."

"Suit yourself." Julie jumped down from the wall about to go.

"Sorry," said Christopher. She paused and looked at him. "Maybe at Halloween?" he offered.

She laughed, then sat back on the wall. "Who's your favourite Beatle?"

"John," he answered as quick as a flash.

"Is that 'cos he wears glasses like you?"

"No," he blushed again. "It's because…"

"Mine's Paul," she said quickly.

"Girls always say that."

"Do they?"

"Yes," he said glumly.

"How interesting…" She smiled slowly to herself. . "Well, I've got to go. Till Halloween then," and she stuck out her hand for him to shake in an oddly formal way.

Christopher went to take it. "Till Halloween. See you."

"Not if I see you first!" And she pulled her hand away at the last moment before running off across the street.

Christopher jumped down from the wall and walked on past Michael's house. He decided he wouldn't call on him just now. If Michael really wanted to see me, he thought, then let him come to me. He swung his bat over his shoulder and whistled as he walked on towards the beach. Suddenly a voice stopped him short.

"Can I come?" It was Michael, leaning out of his upstairs window.

"I suppose. But just you – not Terry."

"Terry's working, remember? His holiday job in Llandudno, deck chair attendant. Are you going to the beach or the field?"

"The field's best, it's a truer wicket."

"D'you think it'll take spin today?"

"Might do. After the rain last night."

"Yeah. A real sticky dog."

Christopher stopped and turned to face Michael directly. "I've got my granddad's bat with me. We fixed it. If you want to play, you'll have to use that."

"Course. That's great." They looked at each other. "Sorry about yesterday – it was Terry, he…"

"Forget it. Come on, it's my last full day today. Let's make the most of it."

"Bags I be Sobers?"

"All right. Are you bowling left arm fast, or googlies and chinamen?"

"That'd be telling. Who are you going to be? Barrington? Graveney?"

"No. I know exactly who I'm going to be."

"Who's that then, Chris?" asked Michael as he tossed the cricket ball from one hand to the other.

"Me," said Christopher, and they ran off towards the field, with the high white clouds scudding across blue skies on the last full day of the holidays. But they didn't care about that. They had all the time in the world.

## Cricket Bats

there are three of them
propped against the garage wall
glowing in the dark

biding their time, these
ghosts of Bradman, Sobers, Hobbs
dog my footsteps still

when summer-time meant
Oval-time and Oval-Time
meant Hobbs, chinaman

and googly, left arm
over fast, leg and middle,
bodyline, records

tumbling like apples
driven through the covers, or
caught out in the deep

till rain stopped play, we
retired to the pavilion,
this shed, this treasure

house of memories,
old score-books, numbers chalked on
slate squares racked in rows

an over-sized white
coat hanging on a bent nail,
six small stones nestling

in the side pocket,
I trace their shape through the cloth,
turn each in my hand…

one to come, over,
the sepia photographs,
newspaper cuttings

peeling on peg-boards
pasted on the garage walls,
a roll call of runs –

solemnly we burned
them, all the memorabilia,
watched the ashes fall

in a slow motion
petal shower of memories
like poppies on snow…

when we weren't playing,
for thunder storms, or during
the tea interval

we'd sit and listen
to archived tape-recordings,
mini-John Arlotts,

made on my best friend's
1950's ferrograph,
and relive again

past glories, run-outs,
lbw's, hat-tricks,
off-breaks, stumpings, fours,

straight drives, reverse sweeps,
spectacular one-handed
catches at fine leg

till suddenly it
was no longer just a game –
D'Oliveira*, he

roused our consciences,
made us see the politics
of slip, or gulley

*the first black
cricketer to play
for England*

of doctored pitches,
wrong 'uns, no-balls, skin colour,
and who'd be third man…

we played one last test,
to the victor the ashes,
sealed in tupperware

from my gran's kitchen,
with cardboard fielders we'd made
placed round the boundary,

arcane rituals,
hymns to fallen warriors,
we unwrapped the ball

crisp and new, a gift
from my granddad saved till now,
red as a poppy

we watched its high arc,
our faces tilted skywards
like stained glass angels

there were three of us,
bold, barefoot, brown as berries,
gilded by the sun

hung in that moment,
fine silk spun by time's spider,
caught in its web,

which still I can't snap,
ghosts of Bradman, Sobers, Hobbs,
whose voices buzz like

flies drunk on cider,
polite, lazy applause in
late afternoon sun

there were three of them,
cricket bats, totems, heirlooms,
they glow in the dark,

will not let me rest,
hand-made, first-bought, passed-down, they
hover above me

three graces, the fates,
cherubim and seraphim,
dispassionately

raising their fingers,
administering justice like ...
... Bradman, or Sobers,

Hobbs at The Oval,
driving through extra cover,
or a deft late cut,

like a lover's kiss,
Bombay, Brooklyn, Bamako,
it sounds round the world

and I must follow
if I am to raise my cap
to the waiting stands,

spring-clean the garage,
reclaim the cricket bats and
win back the ashes

# Lost Empires

## 1 India

## Hero Cyclist

*Reputedly 'Hero Cycles' manufacture more than a million bicycles annually. They are the biggest selling vehicle in Asia and in India they are ubiquitous.*

black frame
sit-up-and-beg
he rolls across the plain
an umbrella
in one hand, he steers
across the causeway
towards an unseen
destination –

a tightrope across flooded fields,
to his right the village:
beneath Ganesha's greedy eye
he pays his dues of sweat and blood,
piles of dung dry in the sun,
a world-without-end
of make-do-and-mend
in the hard-baked monsoon mud –
against this endless horizon
hanging heavy in the how and why
he shimmers, a mirage
floating on ever-turning wheels…

the sun beats down
next year the rains
might not come
he measures the ground –
spokes, pedals, chain –
towards home…

this gliding ghost of the fields,
to his left the factories:
gleaming temples to the new gods
(World Bank, IMF, Grant Aid)

whose golden icons on gigantic boards
confidently advertise
"Own your own Plot of Paradise!" –
beneath their shadow on unmade roads
he cycles against unknown odds
no sense of hopes betrayed
in the puss of unhealed injuries
caught, he hovers between two worlds...

no name
only one leg
a balance to maintain,
the umbrella
shelters him, he veers
first this then that way
in faith to glean
a compensation

## Bombay Film Poster

A giant billboard brimful of promise
(guns, gods and gaudy glamours)
luridly advertises
the latest Hindi film from Bombay's
dream factory: hand-painted disguises
(pink cheeks on dark Dravidian faces)
and the messages of hope they blaze
across the brown, polluted haze:
"All this could be yours!" But not hers –
the woman squatting in the trash beneath
the rusting scaffold. In its shadow she
picks and sorts among the dregs
for old, discarded scraps of rags.
The baby on her arm passively
(scabbed, sun-scorched) surveys both
worlds, comprehending neither.
Flies crawl across her eyelids: her mother
neither sees nor swats;
enduringly she picks and squats.
Her own far-off childhood dreams
will never reach those silver screens.

## A Chance Encounter

It is some moments before I see her,
picking my way through the rubbish
that runs through this country like a sore.
She covers her face as if to wish
either she or I might disappear.
For a second our eyes meet, fused
in a silent shriek of pain,
then the pupils cloud: they cast
me out as surely as she has been.

Reeling I stumble on and almost
miss them: four dead babies, each a clone
of the other, packed in a row
beneath her filth-stained sari,
their brown bodies now grey
in the stuffed street-sewer grime –
dead, discarded, untouchable.

A beggar tugs my clothes, I become
engulfed once more in the wall
of heat and noise that is Bombay –
"I change money?" "You want boy? Girl?" –
and as I turn to chart my way
across the teeming, grid-locked road
(taxis, rickshaws, bullock-carts;
the guttural cries from burning throats)
high above, a circling kite
selects, with the keen, sharp eye
of a predator, or God,
the stopped pulse, the shrivelled heart,
and swoops...

                    In the rubbish, privately,
the woman squats and coughs up blood.
It trickles through the dirt and mud
to where her four dead babies lie...

Fires are burning in doorways,
the acrid smell of charcoal,

incense, traffic fumes and
human ordure that drifts across
this city's maggot sprawl.
She is a *hariyan**. The hand
of God is printed on her brow,
scheduled to gather the night-soil,
which tonight will be her pillow.

*untouchable*

## Vinoba and the Three Brothers

*Vinoba, an associate of Gandhi, travelled throughout India for many years after Independence trying to persuade landowners to gift areas of land to the landless poor. He finally set up his ashram by the banks of the River Pawlnar, where carvings from a much older temple site were uncovered. Among the best preserved was a frieze depicting three brothers at play.*

"Beneath the ashram, where white-
saried women renounce the world
to tend my bones and ashes
and keep my sacred flame alight;
on the self-same spot where I held
audience with my followers,
lie the ruins of an earlier site,
at least a thousand years old,
peeping shyly above Pawlnar's
waterline: three brothers sport
along the wall undefiled,
preserved in stone, though mocked by time's marches –
lost limbs, noses eaten away,
they yet outlive my dust and clay.

Who carved them? What hand first put hammers
to the bare rock, fashioned fingers curled
like petals, like chains, delicate,
strong? Now different hands from those skilled ancestors
mock the crude artistry, want it pulled
down. No. In and out of time they wait,
eyeless, blind as our prejudices,
saw me, as they see you now, smiled
at my approach. Thus do they ever greet
us. For fourteen years I walked across
India, holding out my begging bowl,
steadfastly refused all pleas to eat,
except crumbs of land, the fat cats' crust,
this slice of hard-baked Deccan dust –

and alighted here, this bridge, in the white
heat of post-Partition. The black crows called,
mocking and raucous, as we crept across.
Why here? Why not. Dharma. Fate.
Their ghosts in dreams and shadows I beheld,
as when I traced with stiffened fingers
where once a face was, now is not:
'We are those you shut away and killed';
they serve me still, for they are mirrors –
look, so that you will not forget
when you leave here. My women hold
their meetings on the ghats, offering prayers
for your journey. The brothers endure,
like lepers, with bodies broken but spirits pure."

## Bharat Mata

*In fields throughout the Deccan villagers drape
lengths of sari cloth over bushes to represent women
working – the Indian equivalent of scarecrows.
They are much more effective, for they are
startlingly life-like and, from them, there emanates
a powerful presence.*

patient as the land
she waits, her sari
the colour of burnt
orange, she is there,
a lone sentinel
protecting the field
from pigs, jackals, crows

ancient as the years
performs her puja
as the heat rises
from the earth, the breath
of some wakening
beast, and the morning
gathers itself, slow
and sure in the folds
of her clothes; bullocks,
gently coaxed – cush, cush –
by the gnarled drivers
(hands like shrivelled prunes)
as if to pigeons,
tread the dry furrow,
nod as they pass her,
mother, friend, she scans
the baking plateau

old men clear their throats,
bulbuls sing in the
bleached tamarind trees –

the rituals of
the day are starting:
women light the fires,
wood-smoke coils in the
blackened kitchens as
bare, bold children chase
the long-tailed monkeys,
who chatter, screech, throw
stones, but not at her –
untouchable, she
watches all of this

still, silent, only
her scarf trembling in
a hot breath of wind
mocking as it dies,
the sun climbs the sky
and still she waits, her
shadow shortening,
the horizon haze
pants like a dog's tongue,
chillies dry on baked
rooftops, flies crawl on
babies, while women
shake the sorghum through
vast sieves that showers
in a fine white dust
settling like a skin

throughout the long day
she waits, the goatherds
from the next field call
to her, bells sounding
the miles, butterflies
bask on the parched stones,
water-buffaloes
loom, cataract-eyed,
black hides caked with mud
from the dried field wells,
each clouded vision

seeks her out – she notes
them too, wrapping them
in her expanding
embrace as the sky
reddens; cicadas
call the women home
from fields, splashes of
colour star the land,
yellow, green, orange,
the slow procession,
waterpots on heads,
moves to the rhythm
of the ebbing day;
the bullocks, heavy-
-footed with fatigue,
are tethered to posts,
carts unhitched and sacks
of rice thrown to where
the rats writhe waiting,
puffed snakes waken and
glide…
                but she is safe,
secret as the night
she sleeps, the darkness
cloaks her shoulders, her
face towards the moon –
an auspicious smile
creeps across her lips –
tomorrow's planting
will go well, she makes
her offering, the
Deccan's deity,
incense, water, grain;
toads fart, fruit bats fly
and the wild dogs howl

ancient as the years
performs her puja
and the earth exhales
a deep sigh, her ghost

walks round the village –
each house she touches,
each hope she blesses

patient as the land
she waits, will always
wait, in hearts, in dreams
she waits, watches, waits –
the Bharat Mata*

*Mother India, a
unifying goddess for both
Hindu and Moslem*

## Sophie and Gita

Sophie has everything:
money, good looks, a tan,
a career back home waiting for her.
Today she is walking the wards –
her parents would like to have stopped her;
for what is she trying to prove
with this endless need to be on the move?
Respectfully she follows the doctor
on his rounds who, not having the English words,
describes, instead, procedure;
shrugs to say, "we do what we can…"
but Sophie is not listening.

Gita has nothing:
no money, soon her looks will go,
no one back home waiting for her.
Today she is sitting in bed –
her husband will never visit her;
he has taken away their child
for fear of it being defiled;
when he first saw the marks he hit her –
to him she is already dead.
The lightening skin of the leper
tells the doctor all he needs to know…
but Gita is not listening.

Gita is looking at Sophie.
She has never seen anyone so beautiful.
What is she doing here?
Why should she want to see me?
Surely she must realise,
I have nothing,
she has everything –
she must, must realise…

Sophie is looking at Gita.
She knows she could never be so dutiful.
She is frightened to draw near:
I don't want to, she might see

my words are full of lies:
she has nothing,
I have everything –
yet there is such light in those eyes…

Later, sleepless, in the hot Deccan night,
Sophie tosses beneath her mosquito net,
Gita lies contemplative and still:
her eyes are stars, they look down and fill
Sophie with their secret inner light,
yet they will already be shut
by the time Sophie next sees them, but
their brilliance she will not forget.

Sophie has nothing –
her head is a dream
embracing all the world:
to her, Gita has everything –
a heart that is home
to all that is in the world.

For Sophie it is time to leave:
she continues to travel –
the horizon expands
as each new whim commands;
while Gita is put to weave:
she must learn to unravel
the twisted, tangled strands
with what remains of her hands.
New York, Goa, Mexico –
names that trip from Sophie's tongue
as easy as a blackbird's song –
beyond Gita's capacity to know,
for Sophie has everything,
Gita has nothing.

Sophie's mother tries to call her
whenever Sophie's back in town.
She persistently harries
her with questions and demands:

when is she going to settle down?
Sophie tries to forestall her,
the answers come out pat: when she marries
she will wear a simple dress of pure
silk spun by Gita in Dattapur.
Each deliberately misunderstands
the other's urgent need.

Each year the world gets smaller –
Sophie flies from Delhi to Paris
in less than half the time
it takes Gita to weave her length of cloth.
Gita's eyes are drawn to the wall where
she pins Sophie's picture, a talis-
-man, like the letter she carries
with her always, though she cannot read
it: each serves to remind
them both.

Gita's world has shrunk to one room,
a hospital bed, her loom:
the shuttle flies forward and back,
the endless round, the clickety-clack
of Sophie's heels across a restaurant floor
(a million miles from Dattapur).
She takes her purse to pay the waiter
and sees, peeping shyly from behind her credit card,
Gita, and her old wanderlust returns...

Like hunger in the belly, it burns –
a lost child in Aurangabad
begs, stuffs dirt into its mouth
and wonders if today, or maybe later,
its half-remembered mother might come back –
rich meets poor, north meets south.

Sophie throws back her head in the shower to sing,
Gita pauses, taking up the slack.
To each the other has everything –
*"I'm coming... I'm coming... I'm coming..."*

# Lost Empires

## 2 Mali

## Land Cruisers

After the chaos of Bamako –
its shanty crawl and sprawl
in the shadow of corporate high-rise where
mud-built shacks with corrugated roofs,
crazy cartoons, contemporary cave art
daubed on walls in reds and greens,
nudge and jab at us from all sides,
jostle and grab us at every turn,
*Espace de Beauté* by an open sewer,
*California Coiffeure, Défence D'Uriner*
(though all evidence to the contrary);
as we edge our way upstream inch by inch
against this human tidal wave,
a heady mix of adrenalin and despair,
*Man proposes, God disposes* –
we at last break through, coming up for air,
a check point of rusting oil drums,
out of the city, out on the open road once more.

This new road, this 21st century road,
built just two years ago, for the African
Cup of Nations Soccer Tournament, now empty,
its black tarmac spilling like an oil slick
onto the browns, reds and ochres of the bush,
spawning its brood of black plastic
everywhere it passes, their mouths an ever-open,
always hungry howl, swallowing trees and thickets whole,
their sticky black scrabbling fingers tearing all they touch;
the wind whips through them like a rattle,
cheering when crowds roar "Goal!"
in this soccer-crazed, aid-starved country…

\*

The 4 x 4's we are travelling in
are called Land Cruisers.
It's a good name, for it does feel like
we are in a ship, or a hovercraft
perhaps, floating above this black oil slick

in our air-conditioned cocoon,
cushioned from contact with "the
real Africa".
                    The real Africa
exists by our side, a dusty track
following the same path. Parallel
lines that stretch to infinity, but never
meet.
              It is there, on the track,
that donkeys pull carts laden with millet;
where whole families cling to a patched up scooter
like so much jetsam flung in our wake;
where children bowl with sticks worn truck tyres
as they walk their way to school,
goats scratch themselves on termite mounds,
whole villages harvest the white cassava,
and a bare-breasted woman weeps
beneath a broken weaver bird's nest;
where old men squat below the baobab trees,
the upside down trees, whose roots seem to grow
from their heads in this topsy-turvy land,
as we float by.
                  People wave, we wave back -
each other's mirage…

          \*

Some hours later we have broken down.
Our drivers argue over what we should do,
then settle down for a roadside brew
of Tuareg tea. They pour the heated water
from pot to glass, and glass to pot,
till the consistency is just right.
As we are drinking and laughing together,
we are interrupted by new sounds –
whooping, high-pitched voices
and the rapping of metal spoons on
kalabash bowls – and there, running
towards us along the timeless track,

their shapes materialising out of the
haze, almost as if they've been
beamed down from the *Enterprise*,
comes a troupe of some dozen boys.
They are, I should guess, 9 or 10 years old,
though out here it's hard to be sure.
They're wearing their Sunday Suits,
matching T- shirts and shorts
in the reds and greens of Mali's flag,
more crazy cartoons, soccer heroes,
a little league of Oliver Twists –
please, Sir, I want some more –
but they're too clean to be beggars,
and they appear to have nothing to sell.
Our drivers leave aside their tea to explain.
"Couper," says one of them, making a great
mime and show with his fingers like scissors.
"Couper." Of course. To cut. And it dawns on us:
these boys are about to be circumcised.
The kalabash bowls are for collecting money to
pay for the feast that will precede the ritual.
The village blacksmith will perform the act,
swiftly and delicately, as if pulling a thorn from
a donkey's hoof, they'll hardly feel a thing,
our drivers tell us, before they roar with laughter,
spraying their tea into the dust – they've all
been through this themselves – while we
duly pay up and cross our legs.  After
the ceremony the boys will be packed off
into the bush with nothing but each other
for forty-eight hours to survive as best they can.
Safety in numbers, says one of our drivers,
but we know, as we look around us
at the endlessly stretching plain, that
we wouldn't last five minutes. Like as not
we'd run back to the slick-black road
hollering like schoolboys, hoping to
catch a ride with a passing 4 x 4.

\*

As if to underline the point,
at precisely that moment,
a lone jackal lollops along the track
towards us. He seems mythical,
like a beast from another age –
even the Tuareg pause as he passes.
It's rare to see one this close to the road,
but his yellow-eyed, loose-tongued
stare takes us all in, as if to say:
"Just step a little further
from the safety of your road
and you're in *my* domain".
He cocks his leg to mark his territory
along the back of our Land Cruiser,
then ambles away down the track.
He's like the gunslinger from 'High Noon'.
When he comes to town doors close
and shutters are slammed, the sky seems
to hold its breath.
                      When he's gone
the birds start singing again and
we all breathe a little easier.
Our drivers round us all up.
"Allez vite!" Whatever was wrong
with the 4 x 4's is now fixed.
We re-enter our cocoons and cruise away…

## Fly-blown Douantzé

in fly-blown Douantzé
even the children
abandon their smiles

the wind whips the sand
from the Sahara
into armies of

howling dust-devils
that block out the sun
lacklustre, these grey

children in filthy
hand-me-downs, outsized
vests, bare-arsed, snot-stained,

proffer listless hands
"Cadeau? Bic? Tu as
un cadeau pour moi?"

they clutch at our clothes,
our fingers, our hair,
as if some of our

massive western wealth
might rub off on them,
osmosis, today's

equivalent of
some ancient ju-ju,
and we are its high

priests, our T-shirts the
talismans of new
gods – Beckham, Zidane –

ubiquitous yet
unknowable too,
as fickle but as

tempting as the hot
Sahara winds, which
first spewed up this last

outpost, this ghost town,
where the road runs out,
where the known world ends

The Last Chance Saloon…
we eat with fingers
couscous and lamb tipped

on grease-stained plastic,
bones lie under the
table, tossed there by

last night's customers,
gnawed at and scrabbled
for by skeletal

dogs – afterwards we
squat by tethered goats
to shit and then move

on, the children are
waiting still, they stir
themselves for one last

shred of hope: take us
with you, please, away
from here, anywhere

with you, and we do –
a disease that rips
our guts till we puke

them back to the dust –
but vomit and blood
leave no traces here

the next sandstorm, and
they spiral away –
click, gone, disparu

## Statistics (Lies, Damned Lies And...) The Top Ten Countdown

10

According to UN statistics Mali is the 3rd poorest country in the world,
(behind Burkino Faso and Chad).
I don't know what they base these findings on,
or how they arrive at this conclusion.

9

Here's another:
The average life expectancy here is just 47 years.
47!
In that case I'd be dead already.
Yet in Ségou, as the morning market haggles and heaves,
and the women screech like parrots over chillies and rice,
I see lots of men who are clearly older than this.
Which must mean that many babies are dying.
We're not shown this, I'm just assuming. Like the UN.

8

5 times the size of Britain but less than one sixth the population.
Desert in the north, rain forest in the south,
split by the broad sweep of the Niger that
bisects the map like a down-turned mouth.
Lions, elephants, hippos, crocodiles;
jackals, monkeys, lizards, scorpions;
and who knows what snakes?
All vying for the attention of me –
tourist, top dog.

7

Mali is a country (my guide book tells me) made from eight autonomous regions.
And in just two weeks I can see this.

Not just at the border controls where you pass from one into another,
where bored guards wait without rancour
while you proffer the necessary bribe,
but in the faces of the people –
Fulani, Songhai, Tuareg; Malinkè, Dogon, Bambara.
Correction: Mali's not really a country at all.
More an artificial construct carved from the French Sudan,
it has never been a unified land.
Named for a 14th century kingdom,
an earlier invading colonial power,
there are many lands here, many cultures –
we westerners make up but one more.

6

Mali achieved independence from France in 1960,
then spent the next 35 years in a messy civil war.
The Tuareg left for Libya,
where they were trained as terrorists
and returned with kalashnikovs.
Presidents built highways that led only to their palaces.
Governments flirted with Marxism,
printed their own money and finally went broke.
There've been famines, droughts and other natural disasters.
And if that wasn't enough, when there *were* harvests,
plagues of locusts descended to decimate them.
We're talking hardships of biblical proportions here.

and yet… and yet…

5

Timbuktu houses the oldest library in the world
with books and scrolls in ancient tongues
dating back more than a thousand years.

Cheik, our guide and escort, we discover, is a Prince,
a UN ambassador, who's called in from time to time
to broker peace between the eight autonomous regions.

He tells me the story of how once,
during a particularly sticky period,
a local Tuareg leader was summoned by a French official
to Timbuktu for talks.
When he finally arrived he was more than two hours late.
The French official, apoplectic with rage, jabbed
at his wrist, pointed a stubby finger
at the Tuareg's sun-scorched face
and demanded, "Why are you so late?" Ah well,
my friend, the Tuareg is reported to have said,
there lies the difference between us:
you have the watch, but I have the time…

Timbuktu, for so long undiscovered, endures…

4

There has been peace in Mali now for more than ten years.
It's fragile but it holds.
Like the walls of the mosque in Djenné
(the largest mud-built structure in the world)
it needs constant attention.
Each year, on the birth date of the prophet,
the whole city comes together to erect
towers of scaffolding, a city of planks and ladders;
buckets are lowered on ropes;
mud, brought in from the river beds, is dried and cooked,
then hauled back up to the tower's top.
Men and women, young and old,
camels and donkeys – all get stuck in.
The entire edifice is re-plastered
in this sun-dried, baked red mud and,
when the scaffolding comes down,
it reveals the mosque anew,
gleaming in the sun, like a magician
removing the cloth that covers the cage –
now you see it, now you don't –
and a white dove fountains into the air…

This is something that is not done for the tourists,
even though Djenné has been declared a
World Heritage Site – whatever that might mean.
Last year the local Imam had to
close the mosque to non-believers,
when western couples were found fucking inside.
No – like the Festival of the Desert –
this replenishing of the mud is
something that has always happened,
that needs to be done each year
to cement old bonds, re-affirm old ties...

3

*Festival Au Désert. Cinquième Édition. Essakane,
Janvier 2005*

We were sitting on the dunes under the stars,
drinking tea with our Tuareg drivers,
Moussa and Cissé.
In his customary flamboyant way
Moussa raised the tiny pot high into the air,
pouring and re-pouring from an ever-increasing height,
while Cissé stoked the fire.
Bundles of spiny acacia crackled into the night.
I imagined scorpions burrowing beside me and shifted
uneasily,
trying to look comfortable, relaxed,
as though I belonged there. Hah!

We talked, in fractured French, about the music.
Music and politics – the two are inextricably joined here –
like the babies straddling the hips of the women
padding along the dusty tracks with plastic
water containers on their heads,
or peddling fruit by the roadblocks
between the different autonomous districts
of this skriking country, this muling Mali,
little more than a babe itself, scrabbling for scraps
among the ankle-deep detritus of plastic bags

that roll across the bush, where they gather
in fly-blown heaps along the Niger's edge,
or festoon the baobabs like some new genetically modified
fruit flapping in the wind, crow-like,
leathery-winged marauders,
who have found themselves a new home...

I ask Cheik if Mali feels like one country yet.
Sometimes, he says, sometimes...

2

The Independence Flame in the square at Timbuktu still burns.
Cheik tells me how the Tuareg, his people,
came back from the desert with a new slogan:
*Guitars for Guns. Guitars for Guns.*
On stage, on the last night of the Festival,
appeared the Desert Blues –
a super group made from Mali's biggest names in music:
Tarttit, Tinariwen, Habib Koité, Baba Salah
(who sings of education, the need to learn to read –
'Very good, Baba,' whispered an old man
sitting next to me in the crowd, 'very good...')
For the final number more than 30 singers and musicians
stood together side by side
from each of Mali's different tribes,
from each of the eight autonomous regions,
making music, making a nation.

Bob Geldof was there, roaring approval, but
we didn't speak to him, we all knew what he'd say:
*"What the fuck does it matter if you're the poorest,
2nd poorest, or 3rd poorest country in the world?
We all adjoin each other, don't we?
Saharan neighbours...
What the fuck have borders got to do with anything anyway?
Just stop making excuses and give them the fucking money
before the desert swallows us all..."*

The sand blew into the sound system.
The mikes went down one more time
as the singers took their final bow.
We didn't need to hear them, or to
understand their language, we could see them,
standing shoulder to shoulder, arms raised aloft...

1

When we returned to the camp,
the drivers were still drinking tea and smoking.
We sat down to join them, all as high as kites.
Statistics only tell us what we want to hear,
confirming what we think we know already.
We argue about global warming,
desert encroachment, dropping the debt;
whether aid is a good or a bad thing,
which soccer team will win the World Cup;
but here there's one statistic that everyone agrees with:
Mali has the coolest music.

We sipped our tea while the drivers
sang of victory and homecoming
deep into the night...

## Poi

In the absolute dark of the desert
where the night sky feels as close
as a black fist pressed to your eyes
I shine my torch up into the sky.
The beam is filled with a million motes of dust
twisting and turning like tiny dancers.
Far away the Tuareg women ululate,
their cries bending the flames
of fires out on the dunes.
I pan the torch beam slowly round and down
to find a single, shifting figure, a girl,
all shimmer in the dancing dust.

She is performing poi.

Her wrists delicately revolve,
almost as if she is spinning
an invisible, three-dimensional web
around her, as though
an entourage of fire-flies accompanies her
in a glittering figure of eight,
wrapping her head, arms and body
in filaments of silver
when she starts to dance,
laughing and leaping, in and out
the lacy loops of light.

A crowd gathers around her
drawn like moths to her flame
but she dances on oblivious
completely lost to the moment
surrendering to the rhythm,
her body arches, a scorpion
caught in a circle of fire,
on and on till the last embers
on the dunes burn themselves out,
she casts the ribbons into the air
where they hang like a necklace of stars
till they too flicker and fade
leaving a jewelled palimpsest
sparkling in the sand, picked out
by my torch, footprints
guiding me towards home...

## Crossing The Niger

We are crossing the River Niger, steaming in at Number 10 of the world's longest rivers. It is more than a mile wide at the crossing point from where we take the ferry at some unnamed shanty town – a chaos of hustlers and hawkers, buses and bikes, pigs and rats; boys playing football with a rusted can, girls carrying water in plastic oil drums; rotting vegetables, the stink of fish and rubbish, and us – a dozen western tourists returning from the Festival.

We are leaving behind the desert, Timbuktu and the Tuareg, and entering the land of the Peul – river folk, fisher folk – the women wearing the tell-tale scars of blue tattoos on their foreheads, two lines along each side of the temple, framing their faces like speech marks, they stare at us as if to say our whole lives are in parentheses, caught in the limbo between one world and another, between one shore and another, floating down the Niger at the mercy of the currents.

It takes more than an hour to cross it, muddy waters reflecting nothing of the sky, just a hint of what might lie beneath – a bubble here, a ripple there. Fish hawks circle like aircraft, egrets dive-bomb for perch, then both hastily retreat as something darker disturbs the surface. A cry goes up from the ferry boat – "Allez! Attention!" We turn. Too late. It submerges, a submarine at battle stations, homing in on the tiny wooden pirogues, who ply a more precarious course.

Moussa, our driver, seems to be reading my mind. "Oui, bien sûr. J'ai vu les hippos beaucoup de fois," he says. "Inshallah." Once he and his brother paddled more than a thousand miles upstream from their home in Gao to Bamako, the capital. Why, I ask? Work, he replies, what else? And did you find any? Oh yes. His eyes take on a faraway look. But after 15 months they returned. "Ce n'est pas toujours si vite, si l'on marche avec le courant," he says. When you are travelling home.

Still – you have a job now, I say. You drive tourists, like us, across the desert. He shakes his head. Tourist season lasts three, maybe four months, then we must scratch around, or starve.

He doesn't look starved, and he may be trying it on. But who can say? To him we are awash with money. We scatter it about like so much confetti, like the end of the Weimar Republic, then have the nerve to barter, to force down prices still lower.

When we reach Mopti we stay in Mali's only 5 star hotel – there are showers, hot water, room service – while Moussa beds down for the night in the back of the 4 x 4 after a fourteen hour drive dreaming of home and the welcome that awaits him, so different from when he and his brother paddled back from Bamako, homesick, weary, their tails between their legs… These days he brings money and presents, but with a bitter taste in his mouth.

I recall a moment a week earlier, we were driving across the desert, there were, of course, no roads, not even tyre tracks from previous 4 x 4's to follow, even the dunes shape-shifted before our eyes like waves on an open sea. Occasionally we'd pass other Tuareg riding their camels, or herding their donkeys, but otherwise nothing. No signposts. No landmarks. How do you know the way, I asked? Do you never get lost? Not here, he smiled. "On connaît le désert." We know the desert…

Each night at the Festival, after the music had finished, and the fires on the dunes had all been doused, I'd try to make my way the 500 yards or so back to our encampment. Except that I couldn't. Never once could I find my way, not even across so short a distance, in the absolute dark of the desert. The dunes would change direction. I'd trip over guy ropes, stumble into donkeys, or wander off into no-man's land. On the first night I was tempted just to lie down and sleep on one of the dunes – until I remembered about the scorpions.

At last year's festival I'd read that one person in every fifty got stung. One in fifty! That's 2%, way too high for me! No – there's no way I could survive out here, and Moussa knows it. We depend on each other, what's bred in the bone, trading hard cash for instincts. Eventually I made it back to my tent and crawled inside – Moussa, huddled in a blanket on the sand, slept with one eye open, always alert, on guard, while I tossed and turned and dreamt of scorpions.

Now, back on the ferry, we pass settlements along the river's edge, mud huts with red walls, bricks baking in the sun, a mosque; men hitching donkeys to carts, women washing clothes bare-breasted in the water, or pounding the millet in a ferocious rhythm – up, down; up, down – for hours at a stretch, preparing the evening meal. It's like watching National Geographic, or Discovery – some of my fellow travellers are busy snapping pictures with their latest digital cameras, but I can't bring myself to.

There are cultures right across the world who believe that photographs steal your souls – not the kids here, though, who dance and pose whenever they see a camera, who clamour right around to see the image – instant replay – then shriek with glee for more, but several of the adults seem to cling to the old superstitions. They shoo you away or wave a stick at you. "If you want to take my picture, it'll cost you five euros." Not bad for a souvenir and a soul.

But Moussa will have none of this. He snatches my cheap disposable camera, my fun camera, bought for the price of a cappuccino at the airport, and tosses it to my friend. He puts his arm around me and orders him to "steady, aim and click". Moussa and me in Mali, he grins: here's one for your wallet.

## One For The Wallet

Moussa asks me if I have any photos of my family.
I have two: first I show him Amanda.
He is suitably, politely, impressed –
"Ah, comme elle est belle!
And is this your house, your garden?
C'est si vert." And against the desert it is.
But when I show him Tim, our son,
he is completely ecstatic:
he holds the picture close, poring over every detail,
then, to my surprise, he kisses it.
He is so thrilled he can't stop asking questions –
clearly sons are important in Mali.


I ask to see *his* photos and he produces two –
both of his wife and extremely glamorous.
In one she seems very young and I tell him
she looks like a film star. Whereupon
he rolls on the floor with delight,
kicking his legs in the air
like a beetle you've turned upside down.
Later, though, I learn that this younger woman
is not his wife, though he would like her to be.
He is apparently working on the girl's father
to secure his permission. "Et la première femme,
restera-t-elle avec toi?" "For sure." They have three children
together, of whom Moussa is very proud.
So what is going on? It appears that wives
in Mali can be collected. Like stamps.
It's not uncommon, though the other drivers
disapprove and, when they can, they wind him up.


But he shrugs them off. He tosses his empty
cigarette packet into the street, and I think:
his wife will not be so easily discarded –
she will stick to his shoe like chewing gum;
she will roll through his path like the rubbish
this country is sinking beneath. Like debt

they grasp it from us greedily –
for what other choice do they have –
but one day it will rise up and
swallow Mali whole, and all that
will be left of Moussa is a corpse
smothered in black plastic, burned
and mourned by two veiled women who
do not know one another, but whose
photographs lie in a dead man's wallet.


I like Moussa, even though I think he stole from me.
He was thoughtful and kind and he made me laugh;
he loved to sing along to the Malian pop songs
he played full blast on the car stereo
as we sped each day through the bush.
There's not a patch of this country
you don't know, is there,
I once joked to him. He grinned.
"C'est vrai, mon ami, mais Mali –
elle ne me connaît pas, je crois…"


I suspect he's right. Early one morning
I came upon him shaving. He was using the cracked
wing mirror of the dust-smeared 4 x 4.
I caught him frozen, suspended in mid-sweep,
the razor dangling from his fingers,
looking at his reflection as if
at a complete stranger.

## Patric Takes A Photograph

Patric, the French photo-journalist, is travelling
across Africa, trying to photograph different tribes.
He is going to put them in
a book. It will, he says, be
a definitive study. Everywhere he goes he
seeks out the head man in the
village and explains what he would like
to do. He is meticulous in his
preparations. He secures permission, he negotiates payment,
then he sets up his portable studio.

The canvas backdrop is a neutral shade
of dark grey, which he lights artificially
with an arc lamp. The sitter, invariably
female, and always in traditional tribal dress,
poses as instructed – upright and proud, staring
directly into Patric's camera carefully balanced on
its aluminium tripod. After much careful deliberation,
with due attention given to shutter speed,
length of exposure and depth of field,
he takes his picture, then packs away
his equipment and moves on.

                                        To date
he has taken more than five hundred
portraits. He carries the proofs with him
at all times and, from time to
time, he will take them out to
examine them, much as a 19th century
gentleman amateur might pore over his collection
of rare butterflies. But Patric is no
amateur. Photography is his métier, as well
as his mission. He wields his camera
as cleanly and as clinically as a
surgeon with a scalpel, dispassionately dissecting, systematically
slicing, cutting his way across the continent.

I don't get it. These people, the way
Patric displays them, could be anybody, anywhere.
They are dispossessed, out of time, out
of place, out of context. In his
book they will resemble pressed flowers, lifeless,
devoid of colour, but at the same
time redolent of lost worlds, missed chances.

## Dogon Country

we set off at dawn
here at Bandiagara
the light is steel grey

the air is still sharp
we are in Dogon country
a place of magic

a land of legend
where high on the escarpment
the village shaman

squats on the cold ground
scrutinising jackal tracks
in grids of pebbles

placed the previous night
and now as the sun rises
he waits not moving

to ward off any
birds who might stray to erase
those faint scratched claw marks

*he's* the early bird
it's he who catches the first
light worming the sky

he has his answer
he'll return to the village
after we've left him

he'll knock twice before
delivering his verdict
to the young couple

who need to know *now*
will it be male or female
this child they long for

he closes his eyes
we leave him to his secrets…
riddles in the sands

      \*

for more than ten miles
we walk in an awed silence
deep into the gorge

down Dogon ladders
narrow carved baobab trunks
etched with shallow steps

over dizzying drops
we continue our descent
deeper and deeper

the vegetation
in these remotest places
remains rich untouched

as when the Dogon
first arrived here more than a
thousand years ago

there were pygmies here
then look see those are their caves
hewn from the gorge walls

they thought they were safe
impregnable from attack
twin towers of rock

high rise homes above
the tree line unreachable
secure… they were wrong

the Dogon appeared
winged like an apocalypse
with flames in their hair

riding on lizards
the light of truth in their eyes
victory assured

they threw down their spears
the gods had kept *their* promise
they would keep theirs

warriors no more
hunter gatherers no more
settle, till the soil

make the desert bloom
propitiate the gods in
this new Shangri-La...

we edge nervously
across a narrow rope bridge
linking then to now

towards those same caves
where now they wall up their dead
an unbroken line

their ancestors' bones
piled high from floor to ceiling
serve to remind us

that this is their land
shrunken skulls lining the walls
and we are their guests

there are angry shouts
when I try to photograph
carvings on the rocks

or a baobab tree
or markings daubed on mud walls
or women climbing

to fetch water from
Bandiagara's summit
all are forbidden

for all are sacred
every blade of grass every
stone wood leaf a shrine

withheld promises –
is this what we mean by home
a place of boundaries

lines drawn in the sand
we cross them at our peril
ties that bind but choke

a place that protects
and shuns in equal measure
both blanket and veil?

*

we skirt round the edge
of the escarpment to where
the first village lies

it's like a story
like something out of Star Wars
long long long ago

once upon a time
in a distant galaxy
far away from here

clusters of round huts
mud walls conical thatched roofs
the edge of the world

we are guided through
labyrinthine alleyways
squeezing past donkeys

goats pigs and children
granaries and storehouses
roofs racked with millet

every few metres
we stop to exchange greetings
mark time claim kinship

each person we pass
goes through the same set pattern
response and counter

response taking turns
first him then you a highly
elaborate train

of courtesies – first
pause by but do not look at
the person you meet

then let him ask you
one by one in turn how all
your family members

are, your father son
mother-in-law uncles aunts
even your donkey

after each one you
answer fine thank you fine fine
then it is your turn

only when this is
complete can you turn to face
directly who you

have been speaking to
and start a conversation
then move on until

you meet someone else
and the whole thing starts again
round and back and round

all through the valley
you hear the greetings rise up
rapping their rhythm

the tapping of stones
the clicking courtship of birds
hornbills in the trees

*agapo sewa*
*nah sewa yahana go*
*sewa deh dewa*

on a patch of earth
on stilts stands the meeting house
open on four walls

where the men all meet
to fix and settle disputes
beside the carved door

which tells the story
of how Ama made the world
and of how he split

his child into two
so there would be two sexes
from the serpent's mouth

how to make the cut
he had to slice away the
woman's clitoris

it explains a lot
the offerings of blood and rice
to the god's fetish

the house of women
where they go when they're unclean
for five days each month

they don't seem to mind
our guide tells us it takes them
off work for a week

    \*

but what can we say
who are we to question this
it's their world not ours

for a thousand years
they've followed the same cycle
the same set of rules

free from debt or war
locked in their own lost valley
but hardly cut off

no – we round a bend
below this valley of stones
suddenly flowers

in scores of toy fields
shocks of iridescent green
fabled onion beds

seen from this distance
stretching out to the river
more like vats of dye

but this is no quaint
fancy no idle tourist
dream but a cash crop

tons are exported
each year to the markets of
Europe Asia Africa

\*

our guide's cell phone bleeps
he spends half his year living
in Paris London

something in IT
but always I am Dogon
here and he thumps hard

the side of his head
tourist money will build schools
then – what? more will leave

like you? like me, yes…
the village market's buzzing
our guide's brother does

a roaring trade in
cheap transistor radios
glued to young guys' ears

it keeps us in touch
he says with the outside world
the bigger picture

while at the next stall
they are slaughtering a goat
the blood drains away

and with one sure swoop
they rip out blood-soaked entrails
cast them on the ground

watch where they settle
then study them for meaning
the men gather round

phones lose their signal
the radios fall silent
children strain to see

we stand back apart
separate from all of this
watching curious

the old shaman spits
the entrails writhe and sizzle
he nods satisfied

a shout goes up there's
laughter and hand shakes all round
we're noticed again

and called across
home made hooch in wooden bowls
is passed between us

an old toothless crone
offers us globs of green goo
smiling gesturing

try some don't be shy
with stiff fingers to cracked gums
we smile and nod back

hands clutch at our clothes
and teens claim us as trophies
you give us money?

you buy our drawings?
you let us have your trainers?
we fend them off like flies

    *

our guide leads us down
to a still round silent pool
ominously calm

white egrets gather
in flocks by the water's edge
protected by a

wooden palisade
of closely spaced sharpened sticks
but not so narrow

a child might still slip
through curious to know what
it is he's kept from

our guide senses this
keep still, he warns and – wait! there!
and there! do you see?

and we do: at least
twenty pairs of eyes breaking
the water's surface

now our guide whispers
watch and he slowly stoops low
picks a blade of grass

then very gently
riffles the water back forth
side to side back forth

at first nothing then
twenty pairs of eyes become
forty then sixty

and from the centre
of the lake it emerges
its wide smiling mouth

yawns and gapes at us
taking us all in, in a
slow semi-circle

its broad tail rises
scales uncurled in a high arc
before crashing down

then all is thrash and boil
churn and chase and snapping of jaws
a primeval dance

before falling still
blink and it never happened
calm tranquil serene

they are the village
totem worshipped and appeased
we pay due homage

we take no photos
no one needs to tell us this
some things sear the brain

going way way back
further than any of us
can ever fathom

the deepest darkest
dreams from when the world began
was, is now, shall be

    *

but the world's changing
and faster now than ever
what will happen here?

back at the hotel
less than a day's hard walking
the well might run dry

but I can download
any culture I choose from
right around the globe

and the next moment
I can delete it all at
the flick of a switch

a whole history gone
a link to a satellite
the click of a mouse…

   *

it's the final act
at the end of the line it's
the bait on the hook

the lure the prize the
one we've all been waiting for
save the best till last

just one more climb up
rough hewn steps between stone walls
to the dancing ground

everyone is here
the whole village men women
elders and children

it's like a picnic
a welcome break from routine
a party a day out

families pass round food
children chase their tails and yap
like demented dogs

women settle down
for an afternoon's gossip
men busy themselves

seemingly ignored
as they check the arrangements
one eye cast to the sun

a circle is formed
in the central space around
the baobab tree

we sit on the ground
everyone waits, the sun
drops below the rim

of the escarpment –
it's the signal to begin
far below us in

the valley bottom
drums begin to beat, old men
dressed in blue surround

the baobab tree
rhythm and counter rhythm
as they stamp the ground

and then they are here
the masked Dogon dancers
catch the crowd's embrace

some are perched on stilts
some are the sun and the moon
some are wild creatures

lizards monkeys apes
cheetahs jackals buffalo
crocodiles and gods

it's a funeral dance
and it can last a whole week
it tells the story

of how the Dogon
came to be, how they came here
to this valley

to this escarpment
high in the Bandiagara
to make a new life

free from war and debt
religious persecution
shutting out the world

but now the world's here
we get the shorter version
there's no place to hide

a pair of lovers
masked and proud with pointed breasts
and jutting phallus

pass beneath their gods
high above them on huge stilts
to come together

the sun and the moon
bow their high heads low first to
east and then to west

the cycle's complete
sun and moon orbit the sky
axis of power

the shifting balance
tourism and tradition
east west south north

I sneak a photo
it's a delicate balance
the dancers depart

*

later in the day
we are hauled back up the cliff
in relays on ropes

the higher we go
the more accustomed the air
the less strange the sounds

we're re-entering
familiar territory
back in the real world

## Le Bel Oiseau Bleu

But sometimes there are no answers –
one day, on another long hot drive
across the dusty Sahel, a rare flash
of colour catches my eye, a blue

so intense it snatches my breath.
"Moussa," I cry – too late, for it's gone –
"Qu'est-ce que c'est ça, le bel oiseau
bleu? Comment s'appelle-t-il?"

Moussa thinks a while, pauses,
strokes his chin, then grins.
"Un bel oiseau bleu," he shrugs.
I smile. He winks. We drive on.

# The Special Relationship

## Three Anglo American Tales

> Bush saw the special relationship through the prism of Churchill as a war leader. But there are other traditions, of non-conformism and anti-imperialism, running through Anglo-American history, which represent a very different vision of global power to that of Churchill and Bush.
>
> *Tristram Hunt*

## 1. The Waitress from Mass. MoCA*
*Massachusetts Museum of Contemporary Art

When the waitress from Mass. MoCA
turned away to fix my latte
I thought I caught a glimpse of
a slogan on her T-shirt –
not, you understand, that I'm
in the habit of staring
at girls' chests – but sometimes, you know,
you can't help it, can you? I *mean* –
there are those that shriek at you,
or wink, slyly, like traffic lights:
*Walk, Don't Walk*. You know the kind?

*Get It Here! Hands Off! The Real Thing!*
*Abandon Hope All Who Dare*
*To Enter Here* – then an arrow
pointing downwards… forbidden fruit –
*Big Apple – Big Easy – Big Mac*
*Make My Day – Do You Feel Lucky?*
*I'm a Rhinestone Cowboy – An*
*Urban Guerilla – Eco*
*Warrior – Kung Fu Fighter…*

or those that tell you where they've been:
*Bowie – The Serious Moonlight*
*Tour.* (That's showing my age.
But I often wondered – didn't *you?* –
how can moonlight be *serious?*)
They seem to promise allegiance –
were you there *too?* Wasn't it *cool?*
Let's put on our red shoes and dance.
*I've Been to Idaho and Lived*
*To Tell The Tale   Chicago*
*White Sox   Boston Red Sox   The Knicks*
*The Mets   The Yankees   The Braves*

What do they *mean?* What do they
*signify?* Belonging? These
badges that we wear like totems?
*D'you wanna be in my gang,
my gang, my gang? D'you wanna
be in..? That's why I fell for
the Leader of the...* Yeah, yeah, yeah...


*Your turn to share the secret...*


A picture of my Grandfather
rises before me unbidden –
from the time when Masons were still
acceptable, reputable
even – blindfolded, trusting,
left trouser leg rolled up,
entering the holy temple...


and of course, the ubiquitous
*I Love New York* – where the word
'love' is replaced by a red heart –
like those pictograms we used to
get in the comics. Remember?
An eye, followed by a wasp
with the letter 'P' crossed out, then
an 'H', preceding the drawing
of an ear. Have you got it?
*I... Was... Here...* Go on – work it out


*I've Got a Lock of Britney's Hair
I Threw my Panties at Tom Jones
Bill Clinton Asked Me For a
Blow-Job...* Who *didn't* he ask?
*But I turned Him Down.* You wanted
to stand out from the crowd? *Hmm...*
Isn't that what we *all* want?

Then there are those that offer guidance:
*The Trained Mind Can Conquer Hunger*
(Really? Maybe I should try that).
*Jesus Loves You   May The Force
Be With You   Happiness Is...*
What?  The T-shirts can't seem
to agree. *Two Kinds of Ice Cream?*
or   *A Warm Gun?*

                    I never had
any of these... Shit, I did!
I'd quite forgotten. A Native
American stared proudly from
my Anglo-Saxon chest to proclaim...
... *what?* I can't remember now,
something trite about children
being our only hope for
the future. But was it so
trite? I say that now, but when
I wore it I guess I bought
into it, wanted to share
it around. In any case I
left it on a beach in Cornwall.
I read somewhere that lots of us
do that, leave clothes behind us, like
animals marking out our
territory, and not just
T-shirts – sweaters, shoes, even
underwear. It's like graffiti
scrawled on walls, school desks, fences:
*Kilroy was Here. Jenny loves Max –
True! What Do We Want?* Whatever.
*When Do We Want It?* Now.  Now?
Always.  Sooner.  Yesterday.


"Did you say 'latte', sir, or
Americano? Would that be
regular or decaf?"  Her
T-shirt turns half toward me –

*Proud   Of   Our   Dreams.*
Proud of our dreams? Whose dreams? Does she
mean me? Do we share the same dreams?
I never remember my dreams —
do *you?* I once had a girlfriend
who, every morning when she woke
up, wrote hers down, then proceeded
to analyze and agonize...
It was boring, but that's not why
we broke up — no, that's a different
story altogether. Though
I do recall her dreams had
nothing at all to do with me...


But the waitress from Mass MoCA —
what does *she* mean? Proud of her dreams.
If we were all proud of our dreams,
we'd put that old fraud Freud
out of a job. And *all* the shrinks...
I've never liked that word, have *you?*
*Shrinks.* As if they diminish us
somehow. Whereas aren't they meant to
open us out, expand us, like
those flowers you see when time-lapse
photographs run one after the other?
Open, then closed; open, then closed...


And now she turns again, cup in hand,
and walks towards me. "Will there be
anything else?" And I notice
I was wrong. It does not say "dreams".
Not proud of her dreams. But *farms.*
*Proud of our Farms.* I'm thrown. And she
has to ask me again. "Will that
be all?" No, not all. By no means
all.
              I don't live on a farm.
Do *you?* Does anyone? Any *more?*

Evidently they do, else why
would she invoke us to be proud?
Farmers are in *trouble* – we know,
but then, haven't they *always* been?
What's so special *now?* I *mean* –
who's ever seen a poor farmer?
We all of us need to eat, right?
But that's not it, is it? That's not
what she means – at least, that's not
what I *think* she means. For a start
there's no logo, no brand, just words,
black on white, though not black *and* white,
no glib advertisement phrases –
*Eat The View* or *East West Home's Best* –
just words, bald, plain, unadorned,
as if to say, all of us
have them – farms – stretching away,
acre after acre, endless,
as far as the eye can see. Like
dreams…
                "That'll be 3 dollars,"
she says. Cheap at half the price
for a mug of latte and dreams!
I sit. "You have a nice day now,"
she chimes, and suddenly I know:
when next I sleep – I'll plough.

## 2. The Businessman from Buffalo
New York City, 14 August 2003

The Businessman from Buffalo
is drawn towards my accent –
"I guess you're a Britisher, right?" –
to which he starts to thank me
profusely for Mr. Blair, as if
somehow I'm responsible.
This is not unusual – though
I'm still thrown. How to respond? Chance
throws us strange travelling companions.
This businessman – Ray, his name is –
dons a dark accountant's suit and
a Statue of Liberty tie.
(No kidding, it's true, I swear).
He wears his patriotism
proudly on his sleeve, or rather
round his neck.
    (Somehow this is less
offensive than a Union Jack
painted on a soccer fan's face.
Why is that?)
    Ray has to ask me twice:
"Mr. Blair? You must be proud…"
"Well…" I haver. Does he take this
silence for disagreement, or
just plain old English reserve?
I suspect the latter for he
ploughs on, undeterred. A bit
like Blair himself, I guess, immune
to the vacillations of
contrary opinion. "When the
going gets tough," says Ray, "the tough
get going." And he *means* it –
for *real.*

    Meanwhile in New York's
rush hour, gridlock mocks this sense
of rectitude. Cab horns honk,

eyes flash, hands gesticulate,
mouths utter obscenities.
We are screened off from all of this.
It comes to us filtered in our
air-conditioned, metal bubble.
In Times Square the news ticker-tapes
by: Bush, Blair, The Road Map to Peace.
Where *are* we? 8th and 42nd?
Numbers. How can numbers define
a space, a time, a sense of place?
Ray's punching in his own numbers,
speaking to some processed female
voice on his cell phone. What did
we do before the cell phone? How
did we stay in touch?

                      (Tin cans –
I remember constructing
elaborate criss-cross tangles
between our house and next door –
on lengths of string hung across
the street for sending messages,
decoding only fragments,
futile, intercepted, but still –
illusion of intimacy –
the frisson of being overheard,
the leaking to the press).

                      Ray's not
going to make it home tonight.
Nor am I. Though I don't know
that yet. That comes later. After
the bit about reputations.
"The thing is," I try again.
"Yes?" says Ray, all attention now.
"The thing is…" Just what is the thing?
Why can't I just be polite, shrug,
accept his compliment? "Thanks – yeah,
we all feel that way too." No, it's –
*what?* Not that *simple?* But it *is*.

"Back home not everyone agrees…
What I mean to say is…" Come on –
out with it – "there's a suspicion
that somehow Mr. Bush is…"
"No," says Ray, smiling, without
a hint of irritation. "This
is not revenge, no – let's just call
it 'unfinished business'." For one
moment, I swear, I think he's
gonna say: "A man's gotta do
what a man's gotta do." But no.
He simply nods. "We're in this
for the long haul." The long haul.

Outside our driver is swearing
at some street vendor whose stall
he's just demolished in a vain
attempt to gain that extra yard.
"Read my lips," says Ray, smiling,
and we can – all too easily.
"Up yours," mouths our driver.
"Motherfucker," snarls the stallholder.
"Wait –" a voice from behind us –
"I got pictures. Let me through."
A young Swedish guy, a student,
climbs over cases, rucksacks,
towards the door of the bus.
"Maybe we can sort this out…?"
"You see what I'm saying?" laughs Ray.
"The Negotiator!" (Is he
talking about *Arnie?*) The Swede
evidently thinks so too.
"I'll be back," he grins, then leaps out
to the sidewalk's sound and fury
which, for a split second, erupts
into the bus before being
shushed by the door's soothing
slide…

        Ray, in acceptance mode,

expands, resigned to the eight hour
drive back north to Buffalo.
He calls his wife, explains the
predicament, language lapsing
liberally, surprisingly
peppered with fucks, shits and assholes.
"Take Bush – you gotta understand…"
Smiling, avuncular once more,
playfully punching my arm.
"Decent," he resumes, "a man of
honour."
      "You believe him then?"
It comes out automatic
before I get time to censor.
Ray bats on regardless. (Outside
Arnie's taking mug shots). "Why sure…
doesn't everyone?" The cops
are here now, like the Cavalry,
swapping sirens for trumpets,
just in time. They shake Arnie's hand.
"But the one we all admire…" *(All?)*
"… Maggie Thatcher. Boy, could she
tough it out!" Ray is rocking now,
a deep pleasure enfolds him.
"Her popularity abroad,"
I say, as carefully as I can,
"was hardly matched at home." "I know,"
says Ray sadly, as if it
really matters to him. "Prophets
in their own land…" (Movie stars).
Arnie is running up the aisle
to backslaps and cheers. But the bus
remains grid-locked. The lunatics
are running the asylum.
Who *said* that? Who first coined that?
*Have you heard the one about
Mickey Mouse?* No. Go on, tell me.
*He wears a George Bush mask.*
Goofy – and now Arnie's running
the office in the world's

5th largest economy –
Pluto...

      Staying awake till the
small hours to see if it was true.
Portillo losing his seat. Blair
ushering in his New Dawn.
Outside the neon sky mocks that
false beginning. Reputation,
Reputation, Reputation.
The old, familiar battle cry.

Imagine no more countries...

But we have to belong somewhere.
The Businessman from Buffalo
knows exactly where he's from,
where he's been, where he's going to –
home, two cats in the yard, a wife,
a daughter – things worth holding on to,
that *mean* something, worth fighting for.
"Sure," he says, "I got a gun. Hell,
it don't amount to a hill
of beans if I can't pass it on.
You want some gum?" Then suddenly,
like a gunshot, it happens...

No warning, no flicker, just wham –
wham, bam, thank you ma'am!
Blackout. The city disappears
and, with it, the century. We
are sliced from time, as if a
surgeon is cutting out a
tumour. We are in the land of
No-Time. Native American
Time.

      Yesterday I had climbed
to the top of the Empire
State, surveying the curvature

of the earth, slaking the city
like a snakeskin.  Beside me
stood an old Apache Indian,
grey hair tied in a long, loose braid.
What does he *think*, I wondered,
in my sentimental, woolly
liberal way, of the old place names –
*Munsie, Canarsie, Rockaway,*
wet place, grassy place, bad water
place – his old ancestral hunting
grounds? He turned towards me. He wore
an *I Heart New York* T-shirt and
carried a Macey's bag. He grinned
and the sound of traffic roared back.

As it does now – screams, screeching tyres,
curses, running feet, babies,
megaphones: don't panic, stay calm –
*Walk, don't walk  Talk, don't talk* then…
a deafening, eerie silence.

Sshh… listen… it's the sound of –
in out, in out, in out, in out –
the sea, your heart beating, then a
siren, like a muezzin
calling the faithful to prayer.

Allah, o Akbar!  Allah, o Akbar!

*Somebody call 9-1-1!*
9-1-1… nine, eleven…
*Not again, it can't be. Yes – this is
what comes of your warmongering…*

"Wait!" Ray has stood up, taken charge.
"Nothing is going to happen.
It's only a blackout. Let's just
sit tight till…"
               *When the lights go on
again all over the world*

*And our boys come home again
all over the world?*
                    The Dunkirk
spirit – that's my legacy, Ray,
not yours. Yours is a Boeing
flying into the Twin Towers
on the Breakfast News. Mine's – what?
St Paul's caught in a searchlight,
that plucky, Britain-can-take-it,
stiff-upper-lip resistance,
we're all in this together…?
(Except I wasn't there, wasn't
born even… so why this need,
this competitive urge, to
stake a claim to it for ourselves,
to grab our own piece of history…?)

Ray flicks his cigarette lighter,
his Statue of Liberty tie
glows like a harpy –
                    *Oh Ray,
we are your huddled masses.
Let us* out, *we yearn to breathe free.*

It's then that the stampede starts.
It would be nice to think we all
helped each other, but hey – some did.
Ray lifted down a small French
woman loaded with hat boxes
(like Audrey Hepburn – no, like
Lesley Carron in that movie,
*An American in Paris,*
you *know* – only in reverse)
who thanked him politely, her
gloved hand held Ray's arm a moment,
a mouthed "*Merci*" before she
disappeared into the night.
"Take care now, ma'am."
                    I'm not sure
if Ray took it in, where she was

from, I mean. "We're not too keen
on the French right now," he had said.
"Care for some *Liberty* Fries
with your burger?" Then a chuckle.

No chuckles now. Not now. Our
fellow travellers have run amok.
They can't get out quick enough. I
stick with Ray. I've become sort of
involved. He starts to tell me the
story of his life. "Buffalo,"
he says, "is perfect for me."
He loves its straight lines, its sense
of order. Unlike what's happening
now all around us. The papers will
say how calm it all was, no crime,
no looting, just stoicism,
acceptance that this kind of thing
happens for us now. "It's the price
we pay for freedom." (Ray again).
You got to admit – he has a
talent for the not-so-*bon mot*.

The next day the TV is full
of acts of heroism,
courage under fire, pictures
that speak a thousand words, and then
are followed by a thousand more.
The hundreds trapped in subways,
the woman in a lift for more
than sixteen hours, the dog waiting
by the front door, the homeless guy
sharing his doorway or park bench
like it was The Waldorf. Stories –
I got a million of them –
the city that never sleeps…!
Well – let me tell you – that night
it didn't. Don't listen to what
they tell you.
                *Keep smiling through*

*Just like we     used to do*
*Somewhere over the rainbow*
*When Johnny comes marching home again*
*Hurrah...*
          Can you *believe* that?

Listen to me – it was shitty
that night, interminable
and shitty. No water, no food,
no electricity, no
cash machines…
          You want to know
what it was like? Watch the news
next time it shows pictures of
*Eye-raq*. That's what it was like –
an absence of utilities.
Yeah – there were lots of absences…

After the last car rumbled by
and people tried to snatch some sleep,
that sense of the century
slipping away seized me once more.
How long, I wondered, would it take
for Nature to reclaim this place?
For weeds to crack 5th Avenue?
For the Rockefeller Centre,
Trump Tower, the United Nations
buildings to slip into the
East River? For alligators
to crawl out of the sewers?
For the stars in the ceiling
in Grand Central Station to wink
and then go out for ever?

Occasionally Ray will
punctuate the silence with
another story. His jaw is
set, his face stern. "My daughter,"
he tells me, "is a fire fighter.
If Buffalo is out too, then

she'll be standing in the line
keeping order, making the streets
safe. "Why don't you find out?" I say,
but the battery on his cell phone's
dead.

                    At last, at long, long last,
the darkness leaches from the sky,
leaking like a septic wound.
We emerge yellow-faced and worn
to face this new world order's dawn
as discarded newspapers
roll through the morning's mean streets
like tumbleweed from some Western
Ghost Town. The rumours are rife.
Ray shakes my hand. "Have a nice life,"
then heads off down Broadway
like Gary Cooper in 'High Noon',
*Do not forsake me, o my…*
or John Wayne framed in a doorway
at the end of *The Searchers* –
coming home.

                24 hours
later I too am on my way.
Flying out of JFK
the captain's voice begins to say:
"We hope you have enjoyed your stay.
Please fly with us another day."
I tune the in-flight radio
to 'Easy Listening' and lie back…

*Oh give me a home*
*Where the buffalo roam*
*And the skies are not cloudy all day*

## The Skater from New England

*I don't want to change the world*
*I'm not looking for New England*
*I'm just looking for another girl*   Billy Bragg

The Skater from New England
is caught in a loop in my brain –
round and round Columbus Circle
she goes like a lost satellite
floating above us in space, but
she is not lost, she is merely
waiting, biding her time, till…

I was browsing the internet
last night when I came across
this surprising piece of useless
information. Did you know
there are more than four million
pounds of rubbish floating in space?
Really. It's true. It seems there are
more than one hundred thousand
separate objects orbiting
the planet – enough to create
the world's largest garbage dump.
Space junk – that's what they call it now.
Space junk. Did you *know?* Do you *care?*
I can't say I gave it a thought
either – that is, not until last
night. Or, to be more accurate,
the last three nights. That's when this whole
thing started. That's when I first had
the dream. You see, I've begun to
dream about space junk. Although I
wouldn't call it that. Not now. Not…
Let me tell you about my dream…

It begins in space. A piece of
junk is floating towards me,
rotating slowly in silence.
At first I don't recognise what

it is. Then, when it comes closer,
I do. It's a chair.

                      I wake up.
What does it mean? Who can say?
I only know that on the next
night, there's more.
                      I've read that although
the chair seems almost still, like you
could sit on it if you wanted,
actually it's spinning at a
fantastic speed, fast enough to
knock a spacecraft off its course,
yet in my dream it feels like slow
motion. I can reach out, touch it,
but there's something else.
                      Orbiting
around it is a pair of black
headphones. But even out here,
out in the depths of space, thousands
of light years from home, I know
there's music coming through them, from
the far side of the universe –
you can just about hear a faint
buzzing.

           Then, on the third night, no –
I can't tell you that yet, not yet,
that will have to wait, wait until –
it's like the punch-line to a joke,
the twist in the final reel, it
has to wait in line, wait its turn,
till its time has come, OK?

          *

The Skater from New England
is roller-blading down the long
Avenue of the Americas
against the flow of traffic
seemingly oblivious

to the endless, choking stream
of cars, cabs, trucks and stretch limos
that she weaves her way between –
so easy in her body,
an effortless nonchalance
of balance and harmony,
she wears denim shorts over
black and orange striped leggings
and a grey sweat shirt proclaiming:

*Looking for New England*

Her blonde dreadlocks sway to the
rhythm of her motion, headphones
framing her face, inscrutable
beneath her black designer shades,
mixing Mexican with Asian,
African-American,
Chinese-Scandinavian –
the epitome of cool.

I see her for perhaps ten seconds
before she's lost in the blur of
headlights, billboards, crowds and neon,
of store-front mannequins, and jets
of steam rising through vents
from the cross-town subway –
ten seconds, no more, but she
endures, a palimpsest imprint-
ing herself on all she passes…

But not everyone notices her –
the old man on the corner of
6th and 50th stoops to tie
his bootlace and misses her;
the girl stepping off the sidewalk
to hail the cab that will take her
to her date ducks inside the door
just as she passes.

                    Though the
couple in the horse-drawn carriage
on the fringe of Central Park
with eyes only for each other
feel the sudden static as she
flashes by, and pause perhaps
in mid-kiss... aware of some
slight, subtle change of movement
in the air as she flies by.
                         All
around her the city's music
gathers, swells, that old lullaby
of Broadway – *at Angelo's & Maxi's,*
*the hip-hooray and bally-hoo*
*the rattle of the taxis –*
she picks them up, like record sleeves,
then discards them, subsuming all
within her own inner song...

In my mind's eye I see her still,
and strain to catch what drives her,
the rhythm she moves to, the pulse
in the blood, the city's heartbeat.

She is skating the island's length –
from north to south, uptown-downtown,
she roller-blades Manhattan,
stopping time, freezing each moment
that people see her, fixing
her image to the back of
the collective retina...

             *

She begins in the "erratics" –
those glacier-strewn boulders
in the last remaining tracts
of the primeval forest that
the Munsee Indians called home –
the wilderness of Inwood.
Beneath her feet the tribal drums

beat, then on towards The Cloisters
and down through Washington Heights,
leading the Revolution's
rag-tag army behind her,
flags fluttering in her hair,
past the brownstones and the artists
in their smart art-deco lofts,
and on through Harlem, pausing
only for chicken and waffles
at the *Sugar Shack*, before
sashaying through the *Cotton Club* –
where echoes of the Duke resound
around her, bouncing off the
silver-domed mosque of Malcolm X –
the prophet's face stares moodily
down still, his eyes following her
as she passes the *Lenox Lounge*
and plucks from Billie Holliday's
ghost a new strain of strange fruit –
the gangsters and the rappers
regale her with high fives and rhymes;
at *Michael Jordan's Steak House*,
against the winking neon sign,
on-off, on-off, she slam-dunks
a three-pointer right at the wire.

The neighbourhood soundtrack switches
to the salsa and merenguè
of the Cubans and Latinos.
She carries the smells of spices
and cooked meats from *La Marqueta*
to the wide open boulevards
of Columbia and Morningside,
up the twenty-one storey steel
tower to the carillon
of Riverside Church, which rings out
over Grant's Tomb and the Hudson,
to mark her passing. Students
in the Hungarian Pastry
Shop look up from their laptops

and lattes, their filos and
flirting, to catch a glimpse of her –
what do they talk of, these kids now?
What did *we* talk of for Christ's sake?
Baader-Meinhof, Tariq Ali?
*Yes, we did!* Smoking pot, demo's?
That too – *Stop the War! Kill the Pigs!*
- but these kids here? I'm out of touch –
music, films, post-modernism?
'Buffy the Vampire Slayer'?

But she is gone – past *Pomander
Walk* and *The Sturgeon King*, past
*Fairway* and *Citarella*,
to the Upper West Side, where
each December Yoko lights
a candle in The Dakota
to mark John's passing, the flame bends
as she roller-blades by –
                      the Skater
in New York enters Central Park,
past the *Imagine* mosaic,
through Strawberry Fields, she becomes
a blur, blending with the joggers,
power-walkers, baseball players,
and all the other skaters,
joining hands in an endless dance.

I am she and you are she and
she is me and we are all together…

The leaves tumble from the trees,
they whirl in an eddy around
her, around them all, carrying
them back to the land of No-Time,
of childhood, snowmen, and magic…

*sleigh bells ring, are you listening?
in the lane snow is glistening*

A small boy launches his paper
boat on the Reservoir, which
riffles as she roller-blades by.
The back of his neck shivers,
he turns round but sees only a
shadow crossing the water, and
his boat, becalmed, suddenly leaps,
like a salmon, and overtakes
all its rivals to reach first
the other side, where a figure
in roller-blades stoops to push it
back past the Boathouse, Sheep's Meadow,
the Hayden Planetarium
and on to the Wollman Rink where
she treats the other skaters to
a feast of triple salkos –

*walking in a winter wonderland –*

and Joseph Cotton, in heavy
coat and scarf and battered trilby,
finds a woollen glove discarded
on the ice, picks it up, turns it
over – he has seen this before
somewhere and catches her scent
on the air as she glides towards
him – the likeness is uncanny –
and he whispers her name, "Jenny?"
like the portrait, then she is gone…

While the angel that looks down
from Bethesda Fountain winks,
transporting her on the roof
of a red cable car crossing
the East River to Roosevelt
Island, Hog's Island, Welfare
Island, past the prisons, the
workhouses, the hospitals
for smallpox, the lunatic
asylum – all empty now – where

Nellie Bly feigned insanity
and City Slickers ride the 'Q',
she rattles down cobbled Main Street,
down the Meditation Steps,
to the cries of the dispossessed,
and the incarcerated,
in the lounging, listless, madhouse
air. She gathers them all to her,
puts them in her rucksack, then heads
back to the city's rant and roar…

She glides by the Gracie Mansion
from where the city's mayors survey
their fiefdom – Lindsey, LaGuardia,
Giuliani, all have looked up
from time to time, while signing
a piece of legislation –
*Clean the Streets, Evict the Homeless* –
or calling in election pledges,
as she has sped by. They catch that
faint Proustian whiff of times past,
caught on the threshold of some
momentous decision, before
they turn away, shrug, move back
to their desks dismissive, or
pause a moment, pause and wonder,
removing their gold-rimmed
spectacles, to rub with thumb and
forefinger the bridge of their nose,
then look out once more.

                                        But it's too late –
she has already crossed to the
Upper East Side – the Guggenheim,
where she fulfils every skater's
fantasy – yes, you've guessed it! –
she roller-blades the rotunda,
gleefully creating mayhem.
The art lovers rise up as one,
like rooks from the sycamores,

to caw their consternation,
but there are those who step aside
to silently, inwardly, cheer –
the girl at the reception desk
in cardigan and framed glasses
*("Boy, but you're beautiful!")*
stands to applaud, and the black Night
Porter raises a triumphant
fist. *Yo!* She's really grooving now –
and Woody Allen, shooting his
latest film, complains as she
skates through the background of a scene.
"Who *was* that? She's ruined the
entire composition!" he rails,
and wraps early for the day, but
later, at *Elaine's*, or the next
Monday at *Michael's Bar* when he
plays his clarinet, a passage
of once familiar notes eludes
him – he can't remember quite how
they follow one from the other –
she returns to him in a new
phrase, one that will haunt him in the
weeks and months to come. Writer's block,
he'll call it, but he'll know that she's
still out there somewhere, waiting.

She hits 5th Avenue just as
the late night shoppers, the cool young
dudes meet in the bars and cafés
before beginning their street-smart
*passagiata*. She weaves through them,
spinning their laughter like plates on
sticks, kick-starting their parties, where
all the swingers and celebs,
the reporters from *Hello*
Magazine, all claim to have seen
her, the mid-town MTV crowd,
Madonna and Britney, *Sex
In the City*, the midnight

paparazzi wondering later
as they scan their digital prints,
*"Who's that girl, bleeding through each shot?
Somebody get me her agent!"*

In Bryant Park the Monday night
brigade gather for the weekly
outdoor movie screening. Tonight
it's *Gone With The Wind* – she will
leap right out of the MGM
lion's mouth – *fiddle-de-dee!* – before…
*(Frankly, my dear, I don't give a…
Tomorrow* is *another day)*
… heading out towards the Chrysler –
its chrome-plated spire beckons
like a beacon but she gets
waylaid. She hears the band strike up
the first chords of the Overture
in the Radio City
Music Hall – and suddenly
there she is, weaving in and out
of the legs of The Rockettes,
whose high-kicking, painted smiles
tonight seem more authentic,
and on towards the News Building,
where Peter Finch's grizzled news
hack exhorts us to throw open
our windows and yell to the world:
"I'm mad as hell and I'm not
gonna take this any more!"

She emerges from an alley
at the head of a motorcade
striking east down 44th.
She is back in the full glare of
sunlight once more.
                                Years have slipped by,
ticker-tape showers from rooftops,
we are in that innocent age
before grassy knolls, before book

depositories, to a time of
open-top limos from where
a black-and-white politician
waves to cheering crowds, beside him
his smiling wife in a grey suit
with matching gloves and pocket-book...

The Skater eases down 2nd,
past the giant green and gold
Barbara Hepworth megaliths
outside the UN Building.
The sunlight flickers from the bronze
making patterns in the skater's
flecked shoulders, fragmenting her
into shifting squares of light and
colour, the flags of all nations,
suffusing her face and hair.

She zips back across town, back to
where I first saw her, the long
Avenue of the Americas,
the letters on her T-shirt
blazoning their personalised
message (just for me, it seems)
my own designer mantra –

*Looking for New England...*

*

On the third night of my dream
the chair spins again towards me.
The headphones slowly rotate
in the weightless void of space.
In an endless slow motion I
reach towards them, my hands fumbling
and clumsy, my breath amplified
by the helmet over my face.
I put them on. The buzzing
translates into words, familiar,
mocking. I did not expect this.

*I don't want to change the world*
*I'm not looking for New England*
*Are you looking for another girl?*

Her voice sounds warm and soft, pressed close
to my ear, locked within my skull.
*Not* looking for New England?
*What* then? A new beginning?
A new frontier? A new kind
of special relationship?
The song goes round and round, round and
round – hands across the water, heads
across the sky – round and round.

*I don't want to change the world...?*

I am trying to remember
where I have seen her before,
for it appears to me now
that I have always known her,
often heard the rumble of
her passing in the subway,
seen her take shape like a mirage
in the steam that rises from the
vents and grids that pock-mark this
city of my dreams.　　　　And before,
back in England, back at home,
wherever that is, I've seen her –
fleetingly in crowds – or heard her,
a rhythm, a pulse, a track
laid down behind the white noise
that jams the frequencies – sometimes
she comes through, then is swallowed up
again, spat out, like graffiti
on a warehouse wall.
　　　　　　　　I...
　　　　　　　　　　　Was...
　　　　　　　　　　　　　　Here...

*Where?* She's passing the St. Patrick's
Parade by Macy's now beneath
the Empire State. Surely she was
*there?* In Andy Warhol's movie?
Her fifteen minutes of fame
expands. Maybe Lou Reed sang –

*Take a Walk on the Wild Side*
*And the coloured girls all go*
*Do do do do do do do*
*Do do do do do do do*

- about *her?*

                       Looking down I grow
dizzy, the street rotates, dissolves,
and I'm back in England once more…

Manchester, England England

An open top bus parades down
the closed-off city streets, lined
by more than a million of us,
deliriously welcoming
home our heroes, who hold aloft
their trophy, the Holy Grail,
a transubstantiation,
and suddenly she is there.
"This is so neat," she says,
as she kisses my ear." I don't
even know her name. She appeared
out of nowhere, out of a clear
blue sky. "What's happening?" she had said,
while soccer players squared against
each other. "Time out?" Time out…
But she got it when they scored,
the ritual celebrations,
the passion, the ecstasy,
before she floated away,
time out of mind, out of time,

out of mind, out of time, just
one more piece of jilted space junk...

And now, once again, the scene shifts,
spinning back to the here and now,
the trophy that they carry
becomes a saint, a virgin –
The Feast of San Gennara.
Crowds press to get a better glimpse
of her, while high above, along
the row of tenement rooftops,
past the pigeons in their cages,
past The Golden Warriors –
*I could've been a contender* –
looking up through the criss-cross
iron tracery of fire-escapes,
in my imagination
Robert de Niro stalks the Don,
Don Fanucci, the Godfather.
The air is heavy with incense
and sweat, excitement and blood.
A band plays hymns slightly out of tune.
I am distracted, I follow
the procession, when suddenly,
I realise, she's given me
the slip. Just as she did in
Manchester all those years ago –
I've taken my eye off the ball.

All around me a thousand church
bells begin to peal at once:
The Abyssinian Baptist Church,
The Cathedral of St John
The Divine, Salem United,
St. Francis of Assisi,
Riverside again, St. Patrick's,
St. George's Ukrainian,
The Eldridge Street Synagogue,
The Mahayana Temple,
St. Anthony of Padua,

St. Mark's-in-the-Bowery,
5th Avenue Presbyterian,
San Ysidrio, San Leandro,
Iglesia Pentecostal
Camino Damasco, The
Russian Orthodox Cathedral
Of St. Nicholas, Trinity,
The Shrine of Elizabeth Ann
Seton, America's first-born
saint – all clamour together
along with Tibetan cymbals,
muezzins' calls, Javanese drums –
this multi-cultural carillon
makes a kind of sweet discord –
*this isle is full of strange noises –*
that lulls me with its siren call
till the earth splits beneath me
and for a moment I see it
as Longfellow must have seen it...

Within a circle of teepees
a fire is burning and women call
their warrior husbands home
from the hunt, a fallen brave
is slung astride a bison pelt.
His bride of six weeks, already
pregnant with their son, begins to
ulululate, and the slow, wild dance
commences – the Ghost Dance – the smoke
carrying his spirit high into
the night sky where his ancestors
are waiting for him, watching as
the chosen one among them
begins her nightly ritual treading
of the harvest, blessing the crops,
touching each one as she passes...

*Walks around the fields they planted,*
*Round the borders of the cornfields*
*Covered by her tresses only*

*That the fields shall be more fruitful*
*And the passing of her footsteps*
*Draws a magic circle round them*

… and within this sacred circle
the bride gives birth in the grass,
out of death a new beginning,
and a star falls out of the sky.
The dance continues, as the tribe
buries, with the body, hatchet, spear
and head dress, then burns the ground,
scorching the earth with a ring of
fire glittering in the sky like…

… like Manhattan – and the chiming
and the pealing and the calling
and the drumming and the ringing
and the chanting, all cease at once.

*I have often walked down this street before*
*though the pavement never swayed beneath my feet before*

But just as I think I've lost her,
I feel a tap on my shoulder.
I turn around and there she is,
at the corner of 34th
and 9th. She winks, and then she's off
at full tilt once more. She wants me
to follow. Past Madison and
Penn, through Hell's Kitchen, the Gardens
erupt with the primeval roar
of twenty thousand voices as
Muhamad Ali and Smokin'
Joe collide like two tectonic
plates. As Frazier hits the canvas
and the sweat bounces off his head
and a thousand flashlights explode,
the Skater from New England
is caught in Ali's wide-eyed stare –

*float like a butterfly, sting like
a bee –*

        and her black and orange
leggings flash toward Herald
and the Garment District to
Chelsea Market, down to Kips Bay
and Gramercy, to Flatiron –
*Old Navy & Bed, Bath and
Beyond, Ladies' Mile,* and on to
Luna Park, where the skateboarders
are all left reeling in her wake.

She is heading downtown to the
East Village and to Greenwich, where,
in Washington Square, past Hopper's House,
she pauses to look in the window
of a film noir bar, the Night Hawks
are still there, solitary and sad,
over endless cups of coffee,
her reflection caught in the slow
slide of a tear down the face
of a woman in green.

                    Across
the street, in the park, the old men
playing chess pause, their fingers, like
the talons of some gnarled, mythical
bird, hover above the queen –
maybe this time she might be saved –
and she is gone, and with her
the shaft of inspiration
that hangs in the air like the rook
waiting to pounce, bishop to black
knight's pawn, checkmate in three, your move…

And she is taking hers, cruising
by the George Washington Arch,
where a solitary busker
llke a sentry plays his trumpet,

the notes lingering in the air
conjuring the spirit of
Miles Davis and lost ideals
in their half-remembered last post…

No turning back now, she is
crossing Delancey, to Little
Italy, or what's left of it,
what's not been swallowed up by
Chinatown. In Hester Street a
young man goes down on one knee
in *Lombardi's* to propose to
his girlfriend. She holds up the ring –
the Skater from New England
is caught in its diamond glint –
while round the corner at the
*Double Happiness* the ladies
playing mah-jong rap their tiles
to the rhythm of her roller-
blades machine-gun-rattling by,
children shrieking as the water
bursts from fire hydrants to soak them
in the late afternoon sun, which
catches her in its dying light
as she surfs the spray's shoulder.

West now, the neighbourhoods changing
as abruptly as T.V.
channels – Nolita, Meatpackers,
Soho, Loho, Noho, Dumbo,
and on towards Tribeca, where
Robert de Niro for real
sits in the old Martinson
Coffee Building, making deals
with his pals from Miramax. He
raises his glass of Chardonnay
and for a split second, a single
freeze-frame, she is caught in the glass
as he tips it to his lips,
the deal suspended, put on
hold, maybe there's a better
idea…

Time
        stands
                still.

                        She is
approaching the hole where the
World Trade Center used to be.
She circles it once, twice, then
appears to rise slowly into
the air. The twisted metal
skeleton that remains is full
of rainbows in the last of the
sun. She rides the whole arc, her arms
stretched wide like a falling angel
(like Tinkerbell she is fading:
perhaps we don't believe in gods,
or fairies, or angels, enough
any more – we need to stand up,
stand up now and be counted, you're
either with us or against us)
fracturing, prismatic, into
endless replays of herself,
as she embraces the entire
city, which holds its collective
breath.

        In Fulton Fish Market
the decks are slippery and still;
in the old Customs Building, which now
houses the Museum of
the Native American,
without a seeming shred of
irony, the ghost of Melville
looks out towards her, sees perhaps
the surfacing and dive
of his Great White Whale, his Great White
Hope – there she blows! – before sinking
to the ocean's bottom with all
the rest of the city's scrap
and discard, floating weightless, the
space junk of drowned bodies and dreams...

The old Woolworth Building recalls
when it was the world's only
skyscraper. Now the Skater
from New England scrapes the sky
herself, while far below in the
Luggage Hall of Ellis Island
stacks of empty suitcases
wait patiently to be reclaimed
from the echoes of arrivals,
the painful sounds of too much hope
in the tubercular cough
of an undernourished child from
Europe, Asia, anywhere...

The Skater lands on the walkway
of Brooklyn Bridge, flashing between
each piece of fretted iron work
as she nears her destination.
She's receding from me fast now.
She races through Brooklyn in
less than a heartbeat. At Coney Island
she feels the wind off the ocean
as she skates along the Boardwalk,
past the Russian deli's, out
towards Rockaway and beyond.
The sun is going down. She is
a mere pinprick of light
on the horizon, a new star
in a galaxy not yet named,
a shower of shooting stars that sighs,
bursts like a firework, then dies –
her pyrotechnic displays
burn the backs of our eyes,
focusing now on the prize –
will she lift her head from the haze
strung taut as a wire on the phrase
that taunts as it plays and it plays?

*I don't want to change the world*
*I'm not looking for a New England*
*I'm just looking...*

We need to keep scanning the skies...

# Ripping Up the Past

## 2

## The Unconsidered Things

Amanda likes the unconsidered things:
the machine-gun rattle when a magpie sings;
a rusted sheet of corrugated tin,
a plastic bag tossed by the wind;
nettles growing through a shredded tyre,
winter sunlight on a twist of wire.

She collects those things that most discard:
lichen on concrete, a tiny shard
of glass glinting by a disused rail
track, a piece of sacking on a broken nail;
roof-tiles, tree-bark, creaking gates,
sheds, container-lorries, crates;
man-hole covers, silage towers –
she picks them out like wayside flowers
and carries them home, to hang on hooks,
and press between pages of old school books,
like a squirrel burying nuts for winter,
for the dark days, when the sky scarce splinters;
she brings the outside in, so that she might feast
on colour, light, and other treats
where there seem to be none,
a stone, a leaf, a gnawed pine cone.

Amanda likes the unconsidered things,
the things I'd not be noticing
if she weren't around to point them out,
things I might not know about –

I'm glad that she
considered me.

## A Folk Play
Isle of Man


I am listening to the wind
rattling the chains in the harbour
restless it will not release me
gusting my thoughts round and round
meanwhile – in the next room
my girlfriend sleeps with her sister

I am walking the cliffs in the morning
I am pointing out landmarks of interest
the lighthouse, the Chasms, the circles of stone
my girlfriend and her sister
keep their counsel close

I am studying the past
the island's folk traditions
the beginnings of drama in seasonal rituals
hunting the wren, the boat supper
I am writing my thesis
the rain is rapping the window
the mist is thickening
I am asking a series of questions
she is looking out to sea
the clock is ticking between us
in the rented fisherman's cottage

we are strangers
at the ceilidh we learn a courting dance
the locals are watching us
our fingers form the shape of loughtan sheep
our horns interlock, she curtseys
my leg passes over her head
our limbs entwine by the fire
our bodies blur in the glimmer
I am entering her flesh
I am becoming somebody else
I am becoming her

I am whispering I love her
she is shivering in a corner
I am not your mirror she is shouting
her tears on my cheeks are like razors
I will not be one of your ghosts

I am catching a bus
I am crossing the island
from east to west and south to north
it is a journey which takes me all day
I have appointments in Ballasalla
where the last person alive
who speaks no English will see me
I am standing on the threshold
the rain slants in from the sea
nobody answers my calling
curtains are closed to the day
I am listening at the keyhole
a woman is rhythmically sobbing
to the drip of a broken tap

a candle is guttering broken
I watch it fade at the window
it welcomes the traveller's return
but the chair by the fire is empty
it rocks by itself in the silence
the ashes lie cold on the hearth
on the mantelpiece is a letter
she is gone with her sister to England
she writes that she is dead
she can no longer speak my language
she died before I could see her
you are studying the past, she tells me
these are my ashes study me

alone in the fisherman's cottage
I am writing my thesis
I have my camera, my tape-recorder
my box-file of newspaper cuttings
I am sifting for traces that linger

invoking the souls of the dead
I am recording their absence on paper
myths and superstitions
a forgotten folk memory

I am pacing the cottage at night
I see her face in the mirror
I hear her tread on the stair
she washes her hair in the kitchen
she sings her sister to sleep
she is wrong
she is a ghost already
her imprint's stamped on my skin

children in rags and feathers
knock on my door after sunset
they are singing the *hop tu naa*
they are calling the harvest home
farmers tie crosses of mountain ash
to the tails of fattened cattle
with hanks of green wool they drive them
through fires of blackened stubble

I am watching men weaving women
maidens from last year's corn
they are breaking their bodies and singing
they burn on the bonfires like witches
huge on the towering stooks
the children are carrying dead birds
slung between riven poles
they are roasting the hearts on a spit
and eating them with relish

I am building a shrine
her photograph burns on the grate
I remember her tearing my letters
I remember her cutting her hair
I remember her sloughing me from her
these are my ashes study me

we are acting out our own folk play
repeating the doggerel rhymes
who is St George? who the dragon?
who is the Betsy, the Fool?
the poetry is the Doctor
giving back life to the dead

I am studying the past
I am casting out nets in the darkness
I am trawling for stories
I am diving for treasure
instead I find only shipwrecks

I am standing on the deck of a ship
I am leaving the island
the mist magically clears
Manannan is mocking me
I am closing the book
I am writing the last full stop
a sense of relief that it's over

my thesis lies in the museum
covered in dust, unread

## Coming of Age

It was the kind of phone call you had nightmares about:
"Chris…? Is that you…? I'm pregnant…"
I felt my insides being sucked out.
Words stuck in my throat, redundant.
I mean – what do you say? sorry?
stay calm, it'll be alright, don't worry?
Instead, for the first time, a need for prayers.

Next day I caught the umbilical train
up north –
slashed seats, smeared glass, a long tube inserted
into a dark hole. Accomplices to murder
we stood on the platform. "I feel dirtied,"
she said, and flinched as I held her,
cutting the cord, strangling at birth,
we bled in Newcastle's cold, accusing rain.

It's your body, it must be your choice,
I said –
In Jesmond Dene a snowdrop pushed a first
leaf through its iron womb of frost –
the doctor's words still ringing in her head:
"A few days in the hospital
will leave no scars that are visible…"
- just a hunted look, a tremor in her voice.

Killing the child killed our love, sullied it,
made it
mechanical till we just lost heart –
a knitting needle prodding the hurt
till nothing was left. (Had it
lived it would have been eighteen soon).
Picked, scraped clean from that waiting room
we stepped to face a future starkly lit.

Making love became a violation:
she'd retch
as I came. Like Lady Macbeth

she'd wash for minutes at a stretch.
*(Will I ne'er be clean?)* A slow death
from shirked responsibility,
my own insensitivity
kicking inside me for expiation.

                \*

I don't know if she feels the same guilt or not.
We have
different partners now, one child each.
We walk vaguely parallel paths with
contact always just beyond reach.
We see each other from time to time;
we talk; we're friends; but I'm
never sure whether to mention it.

## The Horse In The Yard

Each morning, as the Liverpool to Manchester
train rattled across the iron bridge, I looked
for her between the caged mesh of girder
and sky. Below, where the last derelict
railway arches stamped across the wrecked
wasteland, and the brown scum of the canal sucked
the life out of the city, I sought her;

and there, beneath the penultimate arch,
in a bricked-up builder's yard, I'd catch
a glimpse of her, golden in the grey grime,
sunlight glistening on her flanks, a flame
of chestnut in the morning monochrome.
She'd throw back her head in a silent scream
of shunting engines, clanking chains, the screech
of brakes, and the train, like my heart, would lurch

as it clattered into Knott Mill Station
to face the fumes, the noise, the dirt, the dust;
but above the sounds of demolition
I heard that whinny of exaltation
pierce the pavements cracking in the frost,
shatter stained glass windows in the disused
warehouses, not knowing till I missed
her once, that to see her had become
nothing less than a compulsion.

It was as the homeward train re-crossed
the city, back towards the iron bridge,
framed against bars of rain and steel, I first
saw you, skittering across the carriage,
chestnut hair cascading as you tossed
your head, your eyes met mine, a wounded beast,
cautious, cornered. A falling chimney thrust
its silhouette against the water's edge
in a final, broken, jagged fist;
and as the walls came down I felt a pledge
fulfilled: we stepped out from an unlocked cage.

**First Night Nerves**
we are sitting on the sofa
the overture has ended
the needle sticks on the record
a pause
worthy of a Pinter play
hangs in the hiss of the gas fire
we stare into it waiting for
that small inner voice to say
beginners please
but we've not yet explored
the whole script, stage fright's descended
on us, rehearsal time's over


we don't know if tonight will
run strictly according to plot
neither of us speaks the minutes
tick by
our eyes are mirrors where we check
appearances one last time
before the house lights start to dim
is it too late to back
out, fight shy
of hurried mistimed exits
to the bedroom before we get
our cue, this is our final call

## Acting Class

We have two teachers: the first one tells
us – draw from your past, dig deep. He calls
it emotional recall. We must become
children again, he says, see the world anew –
hang out your tongues to taste the wind,
like a hail storm in summer let colour sting
you... We feel each other's faces, we mime
the blowing of balloons, we throw them up
and catch them, translucent moons
of memory which map
our own rising and falling – like breathing:
in, out... in, out... to trap the moment, now,
before it bursts beneath our fing-
-ers... Bang! I stare as my partner sheds
real tears for the unreal, make-believe shreds...

The second says almost the opposite:
acting's pretending, he stresses, it
succeeds at best in scratching the surface.
What matters more, he says, is the service
to which we put our craft. He likes
to use words like "shop floor", "work face"; he takes
away the aura; calls actors
"engineers", the theatre "a lab"
working towards change. Acting's a job
like any other, he says, it needs practice.
You're on a street, he urges: report
what happens, as though you're in court.
More important than us are the audience –
it's to them we present our evidence.

The first regards theatre as a holy temple:
to enter it we must take off our shoes,
sit cross-legged and perform certain rituals,
centre ourselves, then delve within –
only then are we ready to begin.
The second prefers things much more simple,
like telling stories or reading the news.
He turns up for class in overalls.

Now I too teach acting theories:
today we play the mirror game,
I look into my partner's eyes
and see myself as I was – the same
fragile, fluttering hopes reflected back.
I try to combine the best of both
traditions. Today there are six
students striving to play different aspects
of the same person. They enter with
a piece of chalk, draw a circle
round themselves and tell their separate stories:
one chews paper, one cuts her clothes with scissors;
one jabs, one pokes, one plays the piano;
and one remembers long ago…

Sometimes to live you have to kill,
cut back unwanted growth to get the fruit.
I pick my own roles now, designed to suit
each scene: teacher, father, husband.
Yet behind each mask the same face appears –
a beginning, a middle, but no clear end.

I prefer these images to plot, plucked
at random they contain endless
possibilities: six pairs of hands
reach up as one towards the flies –
a balloon descends, timeless, weightless;
one clutches it, the rest retreat, contract.
Foetus-like they shudder, pulse and throb;
a hush of sea swells in a whispered sob
as the girl with the balloon lingers
in the spotlight abandoned, forlorn:
she tries to speak, no words come out –
a painful gurgling in her throat
sticks like a question: regressed? or reborn?
Today's lesson: different ways to act.

In class a student claims she understands;
politely the others listen, argue
for a while, then look to me, expectant.

I hate this feeling of being their guru –
what do *I* know? All I can do is blend
my past with their future. Of course I
don't admit this. I pass on half-coherent
games and tricks: imagine a butterfly,
I say, caged in your cupped hands. They oblige,
rapt seriousness on their faces,
(the way I once did these same exercises,
now I question their validity).
Feel it fluttering against your palms –
then, when it trusts you, let it emerge
slowly from its prison; coax it to fly…

And, like magic, it unlocks a memory:
in the corner Gabriella bows her head;
what's the matter, they ask, is your butterfly dead?
She turns away, she doesn't reply,
she is thinking back to America,
and a death she knew when she lived there.
She cradles her body with crossed arms,
her method of how the scene should be played…

My own teachers hover at either side:
one smiles, one mocks, while I still pretend.

## When Dad First Died...
… I felt too numb to think about it,
just relief that it was over, thank God.
That dreadful, rasping cough abated
till drugged but dignified he slid
into a final, unbroken sleep – except for once:
two hours before the end he opened
his eyes and saw us. In silence
he surveyed us, a measured stare panned
across our faces, urgent, leaning closer
in case we missed something. (Dead men's
last words are omens).

                                        Unaware
our son, a baby, gurgles, grins.
We shush him, and the spell is broken.
No matter, Dad's flapping hand seems to say.
(All the needed words were spoken
a lifetime ago, yesterday…)
Now, once again, time holds its breath:
our son is silent; his grandfather draws
out one last, long, shuddering sigh
that empties him. The clock ticks. We try
to take it in.

                      I thought, so this is death?
Not a full stop, but a comma, a pause…

## Getting the Knack

Like everything else, I suppose, it's practice:
a knack which, in time, you get used to.
At first we felt a bit like actors,
unrehearsed in lines, moves, cues too.
But now…

from the cellar of our sleep his voice runs upstairs
to the bedroom where we lie half-dazed…
("Is he awake?" "Timothy?")
… trying to fathom the secrets he shares
with us, syllables and consonants so phrased
as to tease our tractability
of them, endlessly exploring, his fingers claw
out patterns from the air, frame shapes
a moment, touch them, taste, then store
away, for later – nothing escapes
him: the myriad impressions
which tantalise and frustrate
beyond the reach of his expression,
like the mobiles that turn, gyrate
above him, slowly circumspect.

We look down – he sees us, grins…
(Were *we* ever so perfect?)
He cries now, hungry. Watching him's
like peering through the wrong end of a telescope:
we see ourselves reflected back.
Our past is his future; his hunger, our hope…
Perhaps we're getting the knack…?

# The Day the Earth Stood Still

## 1 – 10

## The Day The Earth Stood Still
**1**

Can we bake a cherry pie?
Can we turn the tide of history?
Can we stem the flow of oil?

Can we learn to play a different tune?
Sing a different song?
Can we right the wrongs of history?

Can we pay the piper?
Can we can the can?
Can we pass through the eye of a needle?

Can we put a man on the moon?
Can we sing on a star?
Carry moonbeams home in a jar?

Can we split the atom?
Can we break the sound barrier?
Can we put a girdle round the earth?

Can we turn base metal into gold?
Can we fool some of the people all of the time?
Or all of the people some of the time?

Can we pass go?
Can we collect £200?
Can we not go directly to jail?

Can we kill the spider in the bath tub?
Spot the elephant in the room?
Can we find a cure for cancer?

Can we stay on the wagon?
Can we provide universal health care?
Can we let them eat cake?

Can we have our cake and eat it too?
Can we tell stork from butter?
Can we make a difference?

Can we create the world in six days?
Can we rest on the seventh?
Can we carbon-date the universe?

Can we stop the world, we want to get off?
Can we shoot the moon?
Can we save the planet?

Can we wear the ruby slippers?
Can we have a happy ending?
Can we find our way back home?

Can we climb every mountain?
Ford every stream?
Can we solve a problem like Maria?

Can we solve the riddle of the sands?
Track down the missing link?
Can we find the lost chord?

Can we have a bigger conversation?
A bigger society?
A bigger piece of pie?

Can we run for office?
Can we definitely not have sex with that woman?
Can we have our votes back please?

Can we look for the silver lining?
Can we reach the end of the rainbow?
Can we meet our one true love?

Can we discover the source of the Nile?
Can we find the hidden treasure?
Can we believe in different gods?

Can we change our minds?
Our allegiances? Our clothes?
Can we shake the apples from the tree?

Can we let our hair down?
Can we put our foot down?
Can we pull our socks up?

Can we imagine there's no countries?
Can little black boys and girls join hands with little white boys and girls?
Can we come to cash our cheque?

Can we have faith in the rhetoric?
Hope in the oratory?
Charity in the deed?

Can we heal this nation?
Can we seize the future?
Can we bake a cherry pie?

(Yes we can...?)



## 2

the Bama\*
Alabama

the Victory
the Bomb Site

a home
for heroes

with roads named
after generals

Haig
Avenue

Kitchener
Close

\* *The Bama – short for Alabama – was a bomb site in Cadishead, (a steel town near Manchester), where the author went to school and where he played in the late 1950's/early 1960's*

Allenby
Drive

the Victory
the Bama

older than
time or wars

O Bama
buried beneath

the crush of hope
and houses

built since on
the Bama

Alabama
lollipoppa

eeny-meeny
macka-dacka

der-die
dum-a-racka

chick-a-lacka
O Bama

between the barracks
and the chapel

the slag-heap
and the pithead

the Soap and
Margarine Works

Steel Mill
and Tar Pit

the railway and
the canal

lom-pom-push
the Bama

O Bama
the Victory

the bonfires burn
on the Bomb Site

our stamping ground
hunting ground

for cowboys
and dreams

The Wild West
Outer Space

anywhere but
where it was

Pentecost and
Tabernacle

Back Street
Bethesda

Dante's Inferno
the Steel Works

the Bama
O Bama

we played there
fought there

went to school
and chapel there

accepting it
never questioning

where it
came from

where it
led to

*The Creature From
The Black Lagoon*

*It Came From
Outer Space*

and landed here
the Bama

a maze
a rat-run

of back-streets
brick alleys

cobbled squares
railway arches

then out into
a clearing

the Bomb Site
the bonfires

the Bama
O Bama

the heart of
the Victory Estate

### 3

you can see me there now if you look hard
(we all of us carry our past lives with us
like the locks and chains of Marley's Ghost)
tethering my imaginary horse
to the railings by the school yard

I tip my Wyatt Earp hat with my Colt 45
blow across its barrel, twirl it once, twice
before dropping it from my fingers
blindfold into my hip-slung holster
scraping off the Wanted posters 'Dead or Alive'

in case somebody might recognise
this stranger who's just blown into town
I scan the scene before moseying down
past the Sheriff's Office to the local saloon
to drink sarsaparillas; a coyote cries

I look up, it's Peter from across the street
or the Cisco Kid, as he prefers
and this is his signal and everyone clears
this town ain't big enough for the both of us
Wyatt against Cisco, me against Pete…

\*

turn the page, spin the kaleidoscope
past the hopscotch, whip-and-top, skipping rope
the big ship sails down the alley, alley-o
the Cowboys and Indians come and they go

*Bronco, Bonanza, Gun Smoke, Cheyenne*
*Wells Fargo, Rawhide, The Virginian*
*Tenderfoot, Laramie, Wagon Train*
fording the rivers, crossing the plains

desperate to know just how it feels
for once, just for once, to be Jay Silverheels
the faithful companion, the trusted right hand
yes, Keemoo Sabbee – who *was* that masked man…?

mountain man, trapper, staking a claim
for ever the loner, the Man-with-No-Name
with a silver bullet, clad entirely in black –
I close my eyes and summon them back…

        \*

there I am again, with a ray gun
space helmet from a cardboard box
climbing slow-motion up the pile of coke
stacked in the yard, planting home-made flags
conquering the dark side of the moon

or again, though much later, as James Dean
hours and hours perfecting that quiff
the curl of the lip, the shrug, the what-if
the cocky conviction I'd carry it off
this scrawny, pale-faced northern teen

        \*

Saturday Morning Radio –
Uncle Mac's Request Show!

*Torchy Torchy the Battery Boy*
*The Court of King Caractacus Was Just Passing By*
*Once Upon A Time There Was A Little White Bull*
*Inchworm Inchworm Measuring the Marigolds*

*I Saw a Mouse – Where? There on the Stair*
*Davy, Davy Crockett: King of the Wild Frontier*
*In Gilly Gilly Ossenfeffer Katzanellen Bogen by the Sea*
*Que Sera, Sera – Whatever Will Be, Will Be*

(did anyone ever listen to this –
apart from me, I mean, that's obvious –
when there was American Rock 'n Roll to be had
that made you feel good and that made you feel bad

on Radio Luxembourg, listened to at night
under the covers with a torch for a light
tuning the pirate frequency
that came and then went, but that made you feel free?)

No-one at all at school was impressed
when I told them I'd had a special request:
"For Christopher Hubert who's 7 today
who high-apple-pie-in-the-sky hopes I'll play…"

*Like a streak of lightnin' flashin' cross the sky*
*Like the swiftest arrow whizzing from a bow*
*Like a mighty cannonball he seems to fly*
*You'll hear about him everywhere you go*

You can buy all these back on DVD now –
digitally re-mastered, they seem less somehow –
*The Runaway Train Came Down The Track*-
I wonder what happened to Uncle Mac…?

*The time will come when everyone will know*
*The name of Champion the Wonder Horse…*

*

I un-tether him from the railings by the school gate,
stroke his muzzle, give him some sugar –
it's time to let you go, boy, I whisper,
it's time to take our separate ways –
he nods his head, nuzzles me, neighs
before galloping off into the unimagined night


**4**
the Bama
the Bomb Site

bulldozers
giant crabs

with iron jaws
and steel teeth

gouge the
guts and entrails

chew the coke
and concrete

spit the steel
and slag heaps

into huge
storm drains

staunching wounds
and gashes

stitching scars
and lacerations

leaving multi-coloured
legoland to

seize the future
heal the nation

air-brushing
history

but look closely
now and see

we're still there
shadows, ghosts

palimpsests
shimmering

Wyatt and Cisco
Pete and me

and all of us
the whole posse

the Bomb Site
the Victory

O Bama
Ground Zero

in the ashes
of the bonfires

beneath the ruins
far below

a horse
lies sleeping

flanks like bellows
heaving

expanding
contracting

expanding
contracting



## 5

*Listen my children and you shall hear*
*Of the midnight ride of Paul Revere*

The British Are Coming
The British Are Coming

*a hurry of hoofs in a village street…*
*a shape in the moonlight…*

*startling the pigeons from their perch…*
*the barking of the farmer's dog…*

*a voice in the darkness, a knock at the door…*
*the rude bridge that arched the flood…*

*the flag to April's breeze unfurled...*
*that fired the shot heard round the world...*

Longfellow and Emerson
murmuring through this votive stone

*the breath of the morning breeze...*
*the gilded weathercock in Lexington...*

*on the green bank, by the soft stream*
*that memory may the dead redeem*

\*

The British Are Coming
The British Are Coming

Colin Welland at the night of the Oscars –
*Chariots of Fire*, who now cares

or even remembers?
Public school camaraderie

stoking the embers
of an old forgotten rivalry

*The foe long since in silence slept*
*Alike the conqueror silent sleeps*

and other shots ring out
and are heard around the world

Washington, Delhi, Dallas
Sarajevo, Tel Aviv, New York

Lincoln, Gandhi, Kennedy
Franz Ferdinand, Rabin, Lennon

Booth, Godse, Oswald
Princip, Amir, Chapman

heroes and villains
and sunny down snuff I'm alright

"How did you find America?"
"Turn left at Greenland."

      \*

The British Are Coming
The British Are Coming

and continue to play the bad guys –
nothing, it seems, sells tickets better
than a cold-hearted villain

with a cut-glass Eton accent
a vestige of the old enmity
festering in the DNA

*Spirit, that made those heroes dare,*
*To die, and leave their children free*

meanwhile
the Montana minute-men
hunker down in their forests

bunker deep beneath their mountains
armed and ready
waiting for armageddon

and meanwhile
in a quiet terraced street
in Huddersfield perhaps, or Bradford

a devout young man with a prayer mat
makes bombs on a kitchen table –
each turns their face to the sun

*a cry of defiance, and not of fear…*
*and a word that shall echo for evermore…*

**6**
5 – 4 – 3 – 2 – 1
on the screen a flickering cockerel crows –
a prelude to The Pathé Newsreel signature tune –
then a swinging iron bar demolishes
a cinema as it smashes
into its 1930's edifice…
Headline: `Final Cinema in Trafford To Close`

Pathé Announcer (Voice Over):

> Trafford, named after the ancient De Trafford family, combines the former market towns of Sale and Altrincham, Stretford, Urmston and Partington, as well as several smaller neighbourhoods, including *Old* Trafford, where the football and cricket grounds are. There's Denis Law, painted as a mural on a factory wall. And here's the cricket ball that George Duckworth once smacked for six all the way to London. (You don't believe it? Ask this boy's grandfather — he was there when he did it!)
>
> Trafford — just 40 square miles yet, when writer Chris Fogg was a boy — yes, that's him, with the Wyatt Earp hat — there were 20 cinemas there, and Chris reckons he's visited every one.
>
> The first to be recorded was The Great American Bioscope, part of a travelling fair at Hale Moss in 1900. Just a minute — isn't that Great Grandmama holding on to her hat? She's been enjoying *Fred Karno's Circus*, I shouldn't wonder. And who's that cheeky chappie queueing up to take a peek at *What the Butler Saw*? It must be Uncle Cyril…
>
> Now there are none. A few remain in different guises — a roundabout, a supermarket, a scrap yard — these one-time palaces of dreams…

the screen fades, the curtains close
we wait in vain for further cockerel crows…

\*

*The Central* – converted from the former Clarion
Club – "every lady accompanied by a gentleman
FREE" – later the People's Palace,
or Flea Pit, so forced to close…

*The Hippodrome* – with tip-up seats in the Dress Circle –
"for easy passage with nothing to interrupt
your view" of a screen that could only fit '-inemascop…'

during the Blitz the blast of a bomb
swung the image to an adjacent wall
showing the full picture for the one and only time…

*The New Electric Theatre* – opened in 1914
with a separate side entrance "for the cheaper seats"
it showed footage from the Western
Front – and very little afterwards…

*Hale Cinema* – with its mock Tudor frontage
and "full augmented orchestra"
and, afterwards, "dancing in the Lounge" –
it burned down after a screening of *The Towering Inferno*

*The Regal* – "a cathedral of cinemas" –
two thousand seats and five thousand lights
that twinkled in time to the Wurlitzer

organ that rose from under the orchestra
pit to fountains of Dancing Waters
like a scene from the *Arabian Nights*

*The Pyramid* – an early Egyptian
theme park with usherettes
dressed as Nefertiti
and its own in-house telephone reception –
"This is PYR 123…" –

as the Pyramid Orchestra
played live *The Entrance of Cleopatra*
(portrayed by Manchester's Mary Thornley
All England's première senior danseuse)

and the Lido Singers – Winnie & Hilda
*A Song, A Smile & A See-Saw* –
sang on stage three times nightly
before *Movietone News* and *Mickey Mouse*

*The Sale Palace* – converted back
from a "high class roller rink" on
the "best American principles", its fake
30's frontage a boardwalk
of a Western Cowboy Saloon

*The Savoy* – "our Cinema-de-Luxe
showing all-electric animated pics
suitable for all ages…"

sapphire-blue curtains, mahogany panels,
foyer filled with white marble
statues – its final film *Holiday on the Buses…*

*The Corona, The Globe and The Trafford* –
afterwards a car park, a scrap yard,
and a plot of disused warehouses

for a time becoming the depot
for Manchester's Carriage & Tramways Co –
home for more than three thousand horses –

all now gone for good…
*The Longford* –
later a mortuary, then shut

*The Lyceum* –
the "Bug Hut"
or "lie *down* and see 'em"

*The Imperial Picture Palace* –
"the Brooks Bar Bollywood" –
all-singing, all-dancing Cottonopolis…

*The Essoldo* –
formerly *The Futurist* –
when the house lights started to dim
its satin-ruched drapes would glow

wrapping you in a warm blanket
enfolding you in a deep forest
fire of red and green and apricot
a glittering Guy Fawkes Night light

*The Picture Drome* –
(affectionately known
as the "Ranch House")
for it only showed Westerns

and finally the three in Urmston
the three that I went to the most –
*The Palace, The Empress, The Curzon*

*The Palace* – squeezed beneath a railway
arch – would shake, rattle and roll
to the clattering trains above us

home of the Saturday Matinee
the mad dash for the front row
like the scramble for Africa

*Flash Gordon* and *The Lone Ranger*
where we'd gallop our horses up and down aisles
whoopin' and hollerin' and diving for cover
from the usherette – my best friend's older sister –

who sometimes, while we were sitting on benches,
eyes on the screen, a sweet half-way to our mouths,
would stealthily creep upon us

with a window-pole, towel-wrapped tight to one end,
which she'd stretch along the front row's length
to whack the backs of our heads…

*The Empress* – green and gold
with its dome like a mosque's
and its penchant for holy epics

*The Ten Commandments, Ben Hur,
King of Kings, Samson & Delilah
Barabas, The Robe, Solomon & Sheba
The Greatest Story Ever Told*

- torn down like the temple to make way
for a *Tesco* with no Charlton Heston
to hold back the Pharaohs or part the Red Sea

and, last but not least, *The Curzon* –
with blue butterflies on its gold curtains
and back-row double-seats for courting couples
(where I snogged Susan Holmes through *Gone With The Wind*

"Can I see you again?" I ask as the last bus pulls
in – the night seems ablaze, like Atlanta.
"Well I'm sure I don't know," she replies with a grin.
"Tomorrow is another day…")

and now it's another day for *The Curzon* too –
the final cinema in Trafford to close
*Mamma Mia* and *Hellboy 2* –
the gold curtains came down for the last
time and the blue butterflies folded their wings

(on stage a ghostly couple sings –
echoes of my parents from earlier days –
*Have You Seen My Lady…?
The Boy I Love Is Looking Down On Me…*)

and the last two patrons to leave
had, flustered, returned to retrieve
a forgotten scarf and a last look round
at its darkening, empty art-deco surrounds…

*The Last Picture Show*

## 7

The first film I ever saw was *Bambi* –
I must have been five –
my mum and gran took me,
perhaps it was my birthday.
People stamped their feet and chanted
'We want the film, we want the film'
and a half-eaten bun landed on my gran's lap
which she wouldn't let me eat –
then the lights went down and it all went still
and I was… …traumatised!

No one had prepared me for this:
suddenly it went from cute bunnies
and 'kind of wobbly, ain't he?'
to forest fires and the death of Bambi's mom
to loss and separation, metaphors for
Hitler's advancing hordes,
the need for self-sacrifice… and I thought –
if this is cinema, give me real life any time,
Disney, America – who needs them…?
I didn't go again for two years

Then it was another fairy tale –
*The Wizard of Oz* – and wouldn't you know it,
just when you thought you knew where you were –
Kansas, Aunt Em, Toto and Dorothy –
suddenly there was a tornado
and you were whisked away
to munchkins and tin men and talking lions
and poppy fields where if you fell asleep
you never woke up and a wizard and…
well, that's a horse of a different colour…

But worse than any of these was the witch
who captured Toto and rode on a broomstick,
whose green face loomed out of the screen
and looked directly at me, just me, no one else:
*'I'll get you, my pretty, and your little dog too!'*
That was it – I was under the seat in a flash

and that's where I stayed, not coming out
till Dorothy clicked her ruby slippers, closed her eyes and said
'There's no place like home, there's no place like home'
and we were back in the land of black-and-white again…

*

TV was safer
for a start it was in the living room
and you could always switch it off
though sometimes it could drive you mad
when the vertical hold went
and you had to hit the top of the set
or watch a person's legs
walking on top of his head

we didn't have one
but Pete's family did, next door –
we'd crowd round after school
to watch the latest episode
of *Thunderbirds, The Mysterons
Supercar and Stingray* –
"This is terrible, we're all going to be killed…"
not noticing the fixed grins or ridiculous strings –

then act it out
every day in the playground
till the following week and the next episode –
we spent half our lives speaking in American accents
even as RAF pilots winning the Battle of Britain
or when we were Dan Dare fighting against the Mekon –
America was in colour
we were black and white

then the Beatles came and changed the rules
they grew up on the same streets that we did
they spoke with the same accents we had
and sang about people we knew
places we remember though some have
gone and some might change

25 June 1967, 8.54pm: the day the earth stood still –
the first live satellite to transmit around the world
The Beatles sang *All You Need Is Love*
at the height of the Vietnam War
and the Klan burned their records
on Alabama bonfires…

## 8

a day in the life

she pushes her tongue in my ear
she tells me she's from Texas
she's taking time out she says
will I be her study buddy…?

she's teaching me to drive
putting me through her paces
jumping me through her hoops
you jive pretty good white boy

shift she says when she means change gear
hang a right when she wants me to turn
we're learning a whole new language
I'd love to turn you on

step on the gas under the hood
hey baby you shift pretty good
hitching a ride, taking a trip
a new kind of special relationship…

*

I'm lying on the top floor of an Edinburgh tenement
a crack of light in the granite sky
the night air riffles the threadbare curtain
strung on a makeshift cord across the skylight

the noise of traffic below, the snores and snuffles
of stoned and wasted students flat-out on the floor

just as I'm drifting off I hear a noise
a muffled tapping on the broken pane
a dustbin lid clattering down a back alley
a startled fox, a stroppy gull, the tinkling of glass
and a whispered "shit", then the light foot-fall of
someone landing softly, like a cat –

she came in through the bathroom window –
"Sorry, hope I didn't wake anyone?"
she hadn't, we were all of us anyway far too gone –
except for me… I'm on red alert

she looks around the room
at the bodies sprawled in sleeping bags
like sacks of coal tipped on the floor
she lets her eyes accustom
then picks her way between them
like a ballet dancer on pointe

she tilts her head to one side
scrutinising each shape as an alien might
for evidence of life, for signs of recognition
until she reaches me, I hold my breath
I shut my eyes, feigning sleep
she leans in closer, pauses, sniffs

satisfied she straightens up, breathes
and in one swift decisive movement
peels off her dress and climbs
luxuriously into my sleeping bag
where now there are definite signs of life
and sleep can no longer be feigned…

she said she'd always been a dancer
she worked at fifteen clubs a day
and though she thought I knew the answer
well I knew but I could not say

uh-oh…
she stops…
oops, sorry –
wrong guy

and with the same easy American nonchalance
as when she thought she'd found me
she slips out
steps between the sleeping bodies
in search of the right stuff

wrong guy
the wrong man
the odd man out

the goodbye girl
looking for mister goodbar
the spy who came in from the cold


## 9

```
The British Are Coming 2: The Sequel!
The Aliens Have Landed

1951
The Year My Parents Got Married

(the same weekend that the Festival of Britain
opened along the South Bank —
The Far Tottering and Oyster Creek Railway
The Lion & Unicorn Pavilion
The Skylon Tower and Dome of Discovery
nicknamed the "flying saucer")

1951
The Year Of Living Dangerously

Read All About It! Read All About It!
US Senate Declares Stalemate in Korea!
```

```
Tories Re-Elected in Britain!
Reds Under The Beds — Rosenbergs Trial Begins!
Churchill Razes Festival Site —
New Homes Shall Arise From the Slums
```

but not on The Bama
another forty years would pass
before *they* were cleared –

boarded up, abandoned
the steel works closed down
the big ships no longer sailed

down the alley, alley-o
though children still sang of them
rope-skipping their way down the years

Alabama –
Choctaw for scorched earth…

my parents met in Manchester
in the rooms of Madame Hedevari
a Jewish-Hungarian emigrée
who'd fled the tanks in Budapest
who'd once appeared with Caruso
and who now taught my parents to sing

my father, who every evening
when he came home from work
from the local asbestos factory
would sing a snatch of Puccini
to wipe away the day
*Qué Gelida Manina*

my mother, who looked like Marie Lloyd
who "wanted-to-go-to-Birmingham-
but-they've-taken-me-off-to-Crewe"
who told me the story of *Treasure Island*
every day when she walked me to school
acting out all of the parts…

```
1951
Movie News

Brando Scorches In Streetcar Sizzler!
(Blanche may have depended upon the kindness
of strangers
but HUAC urges the naming of names)

Jimmy Stewart Scores Hit With Harvey!
(the pink-eyed invisible six-foot rabbit
that nobody sees but Jimmy —

                              like the
pinkies that only McCarthy could see
but who testified all the same)

Bedtime With Bonzo!
(where future President Reagan
is upstaged by a chimp —
life will imitate art...)

and The Day The Earth Stood Still — Alien
Spacecraft Lands in Washington
Park (starring the Robot, Gort)
```

    … my parents went to the cinema
often, once a week, or even twice
(mostly to The Curzon,
sometimes to The Empress)
I don't know if they saw these
or not – it was before I was born –
though there were others I'm sure they'd
have gone to: *A Place in the Sun,
An American In Paris, David & Bathsheba,
The African Queen, Showboat* –
transatlantic culture clashes –

but *The Day The Earth Stood Still*
I *know* they saw, though it wasn't till
years later, on TV – I came in towards
the end from cricket and dad gestured
me to sit, it's good is this,

he said, but I've missed the start,
I argued, I won't get it, yes
you will, he said, and he was right...

movie mogul Zanuck,
when asked about casting for Klaatu,
is said to have puffed out his chest,
bit on his cigar and, looking
straight to camera, remarked:
"Who else would you get to play an alien?
A Brit, of course!"
                (Michael Rennie,
later to track down dinosaurs in
*The Lost World*, lands his spacecraft
in a different, but just as hostile,
jungle).
                "Hell, he even tries to claim
he's one of us, passes himself off
as a regular guy, gets to date
Patricia Neale, a real looker,
and then he has the nerve to try
and lecture us, he sends this
robot – Gort – the 'ultimate
weapon', to stand guard while he speaks,
otherwise we'd've nuked him –
better if we had, I say..."

or put another way – as
future President Reagan would –

*a time for choosing...*
*a rendezvous with destiny....*

*are we better off...?*
*do we want to trade freedom*
*for the soup kitchen of the welfare state...?*

are you listening, North Korea?
are you listening, Iran?

                              (Later
the film's director Robert Wise
would unleash a new secret weapon
to vanquish the forces of evil –
Julie Andrews in *The Sound of Music*)

*I am not a crook*
*ich bin ein Berliner*
*there you go again*
*read my lips stupid...*

brown paper packages tied up with string...

*You* decide...
The decision rests with *you*...

                    *


We squeeze together on the green moquette settee
as if we're hunched up in the front stalls
of the Empress or the Curzon
half-expecting the usherette to glide backwards
between us, her wares displayed –
Kia-Ora, Choc Ices, Lyon's Maid...
I shut my eyes, imagining the adverts
(with curtains closed against the sun)
the cartoons, trailers, newsreels
my mum and dad transfixed on either side of me...

1951
*Coming To A Cinema Near You*
*Our Feature Presentation*
*With Its Own Special Warning*
*Guaranteed To Thrill and Chill*

*They Came From Outer Space*
*A Hundred Million Miles From Their Far-Off*
*Distant Planet*
*To Hold the Earth Spellbound With New Unheard*
*Of Powers*
*The Alien Klaatu and The Robot Gort*

*So Shocking It Could Almost Be True*
*A Fear Beyond Imagination*
*A New Age Is Dawning*
*The Day The Earth Stood Still*

so: the final scene – the movie's closing moments
when KLAATU reveals himself at last, confronts
us with questions we'd rather not face –
GORT beside him, his expression ice

*KLAATU speaks*

to the world's assembled delegation –
military leaders, the United Nations
presidents, popes and law enforcers
a battery of ranked TV reporters –

he talks about the imperative for
security for all, or no one is secure
he tells us we have always known this
that our forefathers knew instinctively

when they made their laws to govern us
and hired policemen to enforce them –
this does not mean giving up freedom
except the freedom to act responsibly…

KLAATU indicates beside him GORT
who unflinchingly, unblinkingly stares out
blank and impassive, his massive size
casting down dark and lengthening shadows

*KLAATU speaks*

we have created a race of robots
(he says) whose function's to patrol the planets
and preserve the peace of the universe,
ceded them absolute power over us –

at the first sign of aggression
they will act at once, elimination

leaving the rest of us, the best of us
free, free from fear, free to pursue

more profitable enterprises –
do as we say, not as we do –
it may not be perfect but it works,
this mutual accommodation…

*KLAATU smiles*

so join us and live in peace
or pursue your present course
and face certain obliteration:
you decide, the choice is yours

we will be waiting for your answer –
while lights from the alien spacecraft glimmer
shimmer in the day the earth stood still
as screen fades to black and credits roll…


and *as* the credits roll my dad nods
goes towards the piano and with
his right hand picks out Puccini –
my mum's fists are balled like she's been
given the black spot by Blind Pew –
Gort's eyeless visage lingers…
*Questa Quella…*
                this or that…
                              which…?

        *


and the poet with his artist lover
a quarter of a century later
like eagles high above the cityscape
look down from their eyrie in Dakota
endlessly record themselves on videotape –
they try to claw back time staving off the fate
that down the years awaits them beckoning
(the candle in the window, the bullet in the back)

on one of other days the earth stands still reckoning
the instant karma terrorist attack –
it will be just like starting over…

and she says:    Welcome to the People's Republic of Nutopia
and he says:     In Nutopia there are no borders,
                 no boundaries, no land even
and she says:    We are all Citizens, all Ambassadors
and he says:     Starting the future out of the now

and she takes a pair of scissors
and she clips his hair back close
and she holds them out towards us
and she invites us all to join them
to cut pieces of clothing from them
till they stand before us naked
two virgins

and they wrap each other up in large black bags
(if there are no differences, there can be no prejudices)
and sing unseen the Nutopian National Anthem –
a minute's silence – a precarious dance
at a slight angle to the universe
their long meandering thoughts
fall like rain into a paper cup
a restless wind inside my letterbox still
the stars hanging in the sky like a mirror ball
one by one they glitter and go out

*Questa Quella…*
                 who is who…?
                              imagine…

and he polishes his glasses
and he sits at the piano
and she opens the curtains to let in the light
and she takes a strip of cloth
and she ties it round her eyes
and she sits beside him knitting
and blindfold she ravels the years

the dream is over, he sings, nothing changed –
except we all dressed up a bit...

*

Woody Allen once famously asked:
"Why do they re-make all the good films?
It's the *bad* ones they should make again,
that would be the smarter thing..."

When Ian McKellen re-made *Richard III*
the US previews were less than encouraging.
"I don't get it – Richard *3?*
What happens in Richards 1 and 2?
Do I need to see those first? And –
just an idea – why not call it *Ricky* 3?
You know – like *Rocky?* That would jive..."

But still they do it, don't they?
Did you *see* the recent remake of *The Day The Earth Stood Still?*
You didn't? Can't say I blame you. Leave well alone.
To begin with they broke the cardinal rule of casting:
they replaced Michael Rennie with Keanu Reeves –
who is NOT A BRIT!
                                Now, if they'd cast Keanu as Gort,
*that* might have played better...

*

I have a dream
the spacecraft lands in a desert
a hot sun beats pitilessly down

Gort steps onto the ramp
and surveys the scene before her
(in *my* re-make Gort is a woman

but like the original her eyes
are a wide rectangular slit)
blank, impassive, veiled

she is wearing the niqab
the full *burka* from head to toe
her arms stretch wide raven wings

but no one is there to greet her
she takes a mobile from beneath her robe, clicks –
later she'll upload the image onto *youtube*

she walks slowly down the ramp, pauses
steps purposefully onto the sand
stoops to kiss it, then rises, waits

a sentinel, a watchtower…
years pass… who knows how many moons
rise and set, rise and set…

the desert winds cover her with sand
the dunes shift and rearrange themselves
beetles scuttle across her

and still she stands and waits
listening to the clock that ticks inside her
like a bomb waiting to detonate

then – suddenly – she moves
she tilts her head to one side
the veiled eyes appear to smile

and slowly she begins to dance
a keen intensity of focus consumes her
a tree bending into the wind

trance-like, transcendent
she reveals nothing yet everything
a single phrase repeated endlessly

raw and vulnerable she creates a landscape
that both lures us in and shuts us out
brimming with danger and emptiness

in her head she seems to hear
scrambled from outer space
the white noise of the century's soundtrack

Michael Jackson, muezzins' calls
vuvuzelas, video games
suicide bombs, stock market crashes

voices on the air waves, panic on the streets
the plaintive cries of sea birds
trapped on oil-polluted shores

spinning, sufi-like, she draws us
into her ever-expanding embrace
as we fall inside her orbit

and just when she has clasped us to her
she stops, drops to the ground –
we spin off helter skelter…

for a long moment she lies there
her fingers claw the sand beneath her
back and forth, back and forth, like the sea

till finally she rises
turns towards the sinking sun
throws back her head and ululates

the sound bounces off the dunes
the wind that shakes the barley
the shot heard round the world

in Central Park starlings fountain from the trees
fly in a flock past the face of Big Ben
a dust storm across the sun

she raises her black raven's wings
shakes the sand from her feathers
and walks towards the horizon

slowly the heat haze takes her
she shimmers in and out of focus
you might mistake her for a mirage

except that she's not –
tomorrow the images on *youtube*
will be beamed across the world

CNN, BBC, Al-Jazeera – they all carry her picture
there are reported sightings of her
in Libya, London, New York

she continues to walk through the desert
the wind blows away her footprints
the credits roll…


## 10

in Timbuktu
dawn breaks reluctantly

like a difficult
childbirth bleeding

through the clouds of dust
that blot out the sun…

I emerge grey-faced
from the make-shift tent

nearby – tethered to
a bent acacia

a goat bleats, a baby
choking for air

separated from
the rest of the flock

flies swarm round its
eyelashes – they *know*

a Tuareg nomad
nudges it with a stick

the flies rise
then settle again

he sees me, smiles
and waves me over

points to the goat
looks back at me, nods

takes a curved knife
from his saddle bag

grabs the back of
the goat's neck and

slices swiftly across
its throat, routinely

holds it up by its back legs
so the blood can pour more freely

mingling with the sand
till the convulsions stop

a brown stain
that will not last the day

the rest of the flock
seems barely to notice

soon he'll begin to skin
the carcass for supper

I reel away…
the camp is rising

the morning rituals
are slowly starting

prayers and other ablutions
our guide gathers us round

we are to trek on camels
to the nearest village

stay close to the flock, he warns
we wouldn't want to lose you…

*

increasingly these days
I feel *un*-tethered

like a balloon
that's snapped its strings

I float above the earth
drifting, directionless

at the mercy of trade
winds I can't control

sometimes these stories
this rag bag of memories –

scraps of film on the
cutting room floor

peeling photos
on a garage wall

cricket bats
in the attic

Brooklyn, Bombay
Bamako

the scorched earth
of Alabama –

act as markers
buoys on the ocean

when surfing the web
navigating hyper-space

feels as unknowable
as early mariners

charting unmapped seas
(here be dragons)

they point a way
bonfires on the beaches –

will they guide me home
or wreck me on the rocks…?

# Ripping Up the Past

## 3

## No More Heroes

My friend said shagging was quite alright –
He liked to do it on Friday night –
Depending upon the bird,
But not like watching George Best score.
Now *he* had goals and girls galore –
I wonder which he preferred?

I nearly saw The Beatles twice –
Each time I couldn't afford the price.
My friend went, though: his favourite bit
Was when John sang "She Loves You – Shit!"
Of all the four I liked John best.
(I wasn't fussed about the rest).
He sang of pain and class and sex,
And wore those National Health-type specs.
When *I* wore them in primary school,
The other kids said I looked a fool.

In '67, the Summer of Peace,
I really got into Chief Cochise –
All that stuff on ecologies!
I thought: "Far out, this'll do me,"
And went to live in a Welsh tepee.
Tuned in, dropped out – went home for tea.

While still at University
Lord Olivier asked me round to tea –
No kidding! How could I refuse?
But I felt so nervous I got quite pissed,
Can't recall what he said, not the slightest gist –
My acting ambitions went straight down the tubes.

Next I plumped for a real old-timer:
Ebeneezer Elliott, the Corn Law Rhymer.
Now he was a really radical geezer –
"Bread not Blood!" Right on, Ebeneezer.
But the more I read, the same old story –
Just another closet Tory.

I never went through a rebellious phase,
No Ho Chi Minh's or Mau's or Ché's,
No, those were my folk revivalist days –
I strode like a figure from Mummers' plays:
Jack-in-the-Green or Mr. Punch,
Who deep down, surely, harboured the hunch
That I wasn't cut out for a night with the boys –
So I swallowed my swozzle and sought my own voice.


I don't have heroes now, they fall
Too easily from their pedestal,
They're scattered far and near.
Like plaster ducks upon a wall,
Whose frozen flight and mocking call
Lead you precisely nowhere at all,
They look away, don't give a damn –
They're not who've got me where I am,
So: "Where do we go from here…?"

## Family Trees

this is a story my mother told me
it's about her great great granddad
who lived with his family on the Moss

every evening after work he'd go
to the family cow, lie on its back
his head between its horns

and teach himself to read, my mother
said her granddad told this story
often like reciting catechism

it was what inspired him he'd say…
now there's a plaque in the Wesleyan
chapel in his honour plus a street

named after him – Albert Street –
behind the printing works my granddad's
mother set up when she was a widow

(before that she'd been a lacemaker) –
all are there still, testimonials
to their endurance (except the cow

and the book) what book was it I wonder
framed by the huge sky of Cadishead Moss
that so made him want to read?

\*

my uncle Stanley never learnt to read
never needed to, he said, he was what
we used to call a little simple
I remember him as a jolly man

with a red face and a high squeaky voice
a bit like Mr Punch he made me laugh
he used words like Jimmy Riddle and
he taught me how to play gin rummy

he never went to school, he'd slip off
to the fields and bring home injured rabbits
dead voles, live adders, which my gran (his
sister) had to get rid of before their dad

(a miner) brought his temper home from work
but mostly what my uncle Stanley
studied were birds – he had a way with them
he ringed them, nursed them, later bred them

finches, love-birds, canaries – he became
something of an expert in them, people
wrote to him from all over the world
to seek his advice, my auntie Ruby

(Stan's wife) would read the letters to him
he answered them all, he was the first
person to breed a white budgerigar
after that he let his birds go free

I remember him at family funerals
sitting in the kitchen with the women
he'd take me on his knee and produce
pennies from behind my ear

\*

all families have their characters
their stories – these are just a few of mine

I tell them to Tim, I pass them on
in the hope that he will in his turn

pass them on to his own children
my stories make him laugh for they're no more

real to him than the imaginary friends
he talks to when he's climbing trees

which he does in the garden, making complex
routes among the branches which he tries

to follow but something always distracts
him, he has to start again, he makes up

new rules every time whistling as he
swings casually from the highest branch

the past does not concern him –
I too follow complicated routes

of my own making, I think I know
the way I want to go but always

something checks me nudging me towards
a path I meant to shun – a pair of horns

prodding me in the back, a white
bird flying across the sun…

## Google Earth

In Copenhagen on a Sunday afternoon
a Japanese student soulfully plays
an Italian folk song on a Hungarian violin –
it's an offer that's hard to refuse –

leaning against a synagogue wall
beneath a giant billboard poster
of a soccer player from Portugal
in the red shirt of a team from Manchester

opposite a Turkish café, where I order a Danish
(except that here it's called an American)
and take a seat in the last available booth, which
is guarded by a smiling store front mannequin,

who is so eerily life-like that at first
I mistake him for real and ask him if
the seat is taken, but he doesn't reply –
he waits while the Hop-on/Hop-off

land train slowly trundles by:
"Experience Purity with a Twist",
its carriages lumberingly proclaim –
the strong, silent type, I think, until

I realise – who looks more at home,
I wonder? It's a moot point – while
atop a civic building at the river's bend
a huge Macdonald's clown beams down

bestriding, arms akimbo, confident,
as if he's always been there,
a colossus, a Mount Rushmore president:
"I'm Loving It!" he declares,

the words enshrined in a cartoon bubble
as far below, a cardboard Viking,
who tips to his lips a Carlsberg bottle,
whimpers: "*Possibly* the best lager in town",

which I, a British visitor, later will recall
in some stateless airport terminal,
set down, then e-mail to my friend
to read in a Massachusetts living

room from where, if she looks me up on Google
Earth, she might see me trudging through the rain
with my cappuccino in one hand and bagel
in the other, scouring these streets in vain,

the song the Japanese student played
still running through my brain, while I
look for the Hans Anderson Mermaid
which I'm told's been shipped off to Shanghai.

## Moon Magic

Moon magic, old magic,
from a time before gods,
we scanned the skies for signs
you still watched over us,
before we gave you names –
sickle moon, harvest moon
old and new, quarter, half,
huntress, blood-red – shuffling
tides like tarot packs,
mapping moods and futures
on the throw of a dice,
green Mona Lisa smile.

As a child in the dark
you sought me out, your face
unblinking, a searchlight
pursuing me between
alleys of blind houses –
I tried to run away
but always you found me
even in my secret
hiding place which no-one
knew about – except you.
I shut my eyes but still
you would not go away…

until my grandmother
peering over half-moon
spectacles, the smell of
molten rocks and nectar
in her hands, explained it
to me quite differently.
She's keeping an eye out,
that's all, she said, making
sure you don't get lost, see,
lighting your way back home –
her frail, cracked voice sang clear:
my Huckleberry friend…

and though at last we came
to name you, classify
your craters and contours,
passing from your ocean
of storms into that wide
sea of tranquillity
where we tell stories, sing
songs, even fire rockets
to try and steal your heart,
you kept your dark side close,
a glimpse of ankle, a
tease of stocking – now you
see me and now you don't

you old devil moon, you –
let's put on our red shoes
and, under your moonlight,
your serious moonlight,
let's dance. Let's climb this last
long stairway to heaven,
wider than a mile,
we're crossing you in style,
last night, in pale moonlight,
I saw you, I saw you,
with moonbeams in a jar,
moon shadow, moon shadow…

\*

In these uncertain times,
you've remained our constant,
our watchword, our beacon;
in the early days, if
circumstance should part us,
we'd both look up to watch
the wax and wane and wonder,
our love arc-ing the skies,
let's agree to meet here –
same time, same place, same thought –
and if we lose our way,
your light will guide us home.

## Potting On

There is a photograph I have
of Amanda in the garden;
so easy in her body she
kneels by the flowers, her busy
fingers thinning out weeds. She is
unaware I am watching her:
there is deep contentment in
the way she works. After a time
she notices me – there is mud
on her nose which she wrinkles as
she smiles. Come and look, she says, then
shows me what she's done: poppies and
cornflowers nod in the breeze while
mallow and marigold wink back.
These have set themselves, she says, her
delight transparent as a child's.

Sometimes seeds lie dormant for years,
becoming little more than a
memory of how the summers
used to be, a child's picture book.
I flick the pages and I find
further reminders: Amanda
in her Sunday best for Whit Walks,
Amanda with an Easter egg,
Amanda with a doll's house and,
always, always, there's Amanda
dancing – the same soulful, oval
face, the serious-sad eyes that
catch at pleasure like moths at night
who beat their wings against the glass.

I flick the pages further and
the years go rushing by me. It's
a dizzy roller-coaster ride:
memories blur like old photographs,
colour fading to black and white,
reducing the image to a
simple basic composition –

a single face in focus, a
blue star of flax in the meadow
peeping from the darkness after
years of neglect lying buried…

I take the dust sheet off all these
memories and shake them in the sun.
One by one I examine them –
they all come down to this one face.
It's the one photograph I'd keep,
yes, Amanda in the garden –
only now she's in the greenhouse
sitting at a makeshift table
full of trays and seed-packets and
the remnants of last year's cuttings.
She is singing as I watch her,
the past tumbling from her fingers
in tiny molecules of soil.
I hold my breath… she is potting
on the future… her hands open…

## Acknowledgements

I would like to thank my parents and grandparents for providing me with so many stories and memories that I have been able to draw on here; Chris Waters and Sally Chapman-Walker of Mudlark Press for their commitment to this project and for their unfailing support for my work; the David Hall in South Petherton for allowing me to try out the Three Anglo-American Tales there as a performance piece to gauge the reactions of listeners, which in turn led me to put this collection together, and 4 Reel Films, Andrew Pastor and Jenny Edmunds for enabling that event to take place; Jo Willmott and Nikki Penfold for dancing and giving the work a fresh perspective; Billy Bragg for permission to quote from a great song and Juliet from his office for the heart-warming observation that "all great art borrows"; Fiona Grundy from Classic Media for so kindly allowing us to use the wonderful image of the Lone Ranger and Tonto on the front cover (Who *was* that masked man?); Tony Smith for first showing me India; Take Art for making it possible for me to travel to Mali; Ros Fry, Chris Huxley, Liz & Nell Leyshon, Subathra Subramaniam, Quentin Cooper and the Berkshires Writers Group New England for reading various versions of the poems and for so generously offering their comments and suggestions; Gavin Stride, who makes me believe anything is possible and who never stops encouraging me; Chrissie Godfrey & Paul Birch for making their own Moon Magic; Helen Burdette for uncovering The Boy in the Wardrobe; Ben Wright for the gift of his glorious dance at a slight angle to the universe; indeed, all the dance artists I currently collaborate with, who keep on creatively feeding me; and, last but by no means least, the poet Irene Willis & her husband Daves Rossell in Massachusetts for their inspiration, friendship, warmth and welcome. There is nobody I know who is more passionate about poetry than Irene, and it is she who, as well as offering so much wise advice, has always urged me to keep on telling stories.

Chris grew up in Manchester and is currently Creative Producer for South East Dance in Brighton, co-ordinating their Associate Artists programme, and for the National Bonnie Bird Choreography Award. He has many years' experience of arts project development and management, especially in the East Midlands and the South-West, and between 2003 and 2009 he was Director of Dance and Theatre for Take Art, an arts development agency in Somerset.

He continues to work as a writer and theatre director, most recently with New Perspectives in Nottinghamshire and Farnham Maltings in Surrey, under the artistic direction of Gavin Stride, with whom Chris is a frequent collaborator, and he now regularly acts as a dramaturg for choreographers and dance artists.

Chris currently lives in West Dorset and Brighton with his wife, Amanda, a dance practitioner working with older people and those with Parkinson's. They have a son, Tim, who is an independent film maker and director of 4 Reel Films.

For further information contact: chris@chfogg.co.uk